Practicing
Reverence

ROSS L. SMILLIE

PRACTICING REVERENCE

an ethic for sustainable earth communities

CopperHouse

Editor: Ellen Turnbull
Cover and interior design: Verena Velten
Proofreader: Dianne Greenslade

SILVER CopperHouse is an imprint of Wood Lake Publishing,
Inc. Wood Lake Publishing acknowledges the financial
BNC CERTIFIED | BIBLIOGRAPHIC DATA 2011-12 support of the Government of Canada, through the
Book Publishing Industry Development Program (BPIDP) for its publishing activities. Wood Lake Publishing also acknowledges the financial support of the Province of British Columbia through the Book Publishing Tax Credit.

At Wood Lake Publishing, we practise what we publish, being guided by a concern for fairness, justice, and equal opportunity in all of our relationships with
employees and customers. A percentage of all profit is donated to charitable organizations.

Library and Archives Canada Cataloguing in Publication
Smillie, Ross L. (Ross Lawrence), 1959-
    Practicing reverence : an ethic for sustainable earth communities / Ross L. Smillie.
Includes bibliographical references and index.
Issued also in electronic format.
ISBN 978-1-55145-593-8
    1. Environmental ethics. 2. Human ecology. 3. Environmental justice.
4. Human ecology–Religious aspects–Christianity. 5. Environmental justice–
Religious aspects–Christianity. I. Title.
GE42.S65 2011   179'.1   C2011-905627-5

Published by CopperHouse
An imprint of Wood Lake Publishing Inc.
9590 Jim Bailey Road, Kelowna, BC, Canada, V4V 1R2
www.woodlakebooks.com
250.766.2778

Printing 10 9 8 7 6 5 4 3 2 1
Printed in Canada by
Houghton Boston

Green
choices   At WOOD LAKE PUBLISHING we are committed to caring for
the environment and all creation. WOOD LAKE PUBLISHING
recycles, reuses, and encourages readers to do the same. Resources are printed
on 100% post-consumer recycled paper and more environmentally friendly
groundwood papers (newsprint), whenever possible.

Dedication

This book is dedicated to the people – past, present, and future – of St. Andrew's United Church in Lacombe, Alberta, Canada

> with gratitude for the faithfulness of those who have gone before;
>
> with appreciation for the integrity of those who share the current moment;
>
> with hope that those not yet born will build boldly on our foundation.

Contents

Acknowledgements

A book is not a solitary achievement, and this one certainly has not been. I am grateful for many who have contributed to this project:

- The people of St. Andrew's United Church in Lacombe, Alberta, for the strength of their community, their commitment to living as a discipleship community, and their support of the sabbatical and the study leaves during which much of the writing was completed;
- Reverend Mervin Gallant, my partner in ministry, for his friendship and generosity, and for his encouragement during the development of this book;
- The students and staff of St. Stephen's College, Edmonton, for their enthusiasm for my course, "Living with Respect in Creation: Ecology, Ethics and Theology in Dialogue";
- Friends and colleagues Sheila Newman, Margaret Linklater, Jim Helm, Pat Juskiw, Bruce Buttler, Mary Lou Swift, Christiane Brouwer, Denise Harmon, Alan Richards, Terry Anderson, Betty Mackenzie, Gail Hughes, Vic Bergen, Ken and Betty Ditzler, David Holmes, Emmanuel Gatera, Ellen Finn, and Lann Lieurance, who offered helpful feedback and encouragement on early drafts of this book;
- Staff at Wood Lake Publishing and Ellen Turnbull, the editor there, whose careful pruning of this work transformed a sprawling weed into a tidy shrub;
- Larry and Doreen Smillie, my parents, and other family members, for their interest and encouragement on this project;
- Sara and Sean, my children, for making me proud; and
- Therese Thompson, my partner in life, for her support, patience, and forbearance while I spent long hours at the computer.

INTRODUCTION

A plane filled with passengers hit some severe turbulence during the flight. There was a bright flash of light and an alarming loud bang. The pilot came on the intercom and said, "Ladies and gentlemen, I have some good news and some bad news. The bad news is that we were hit by lightning and all of our navigational and communications instruments are shorted out. We have no radio, no compass, no GPS. We have no idea where we are or what direction we are going in." The captain paused, and people looked around nervously at each other as they absorbed the news. Then the captain continued, "But the good news is that we do know our airspeed, and we are making very good time."

For me, that joke encapsulates the spirit of our times. We live in a society that is going somewhere very, very fast, but we often have no idea where that is, or if we want to get there. The power of modern science and technology means that we can do things that previous generations never dreamed of. We can communicate and transmit information instantaneously around the world. We can cure many diseases and alleviate painful conditions. We have globalized commerce and trade. We are indeed going somewhere very, very fast. But the questions raised by the joke are profoundly important: Do we know where we are going? And do we really want to go there?

As humans we are not totally governed by instinct. We constantly make choices that affect us, both individually and as a society. Some choices, like that of speed, are technical ones. Others, such as the question of direction, are moral choices. Some moral choices are profound and define a generation, and may be recognized only in retrospect. In Nazi Germany, for example, most people went about their ordinary lives without recognizing the moral significance of the Nazi treatment of Jews and other minority groups. Later generations of Germans look back on that time and wonder how it was that so many of their countrymen failed to recognize and act on the great moral test of their time. Remaining neutral on such questions is not an option. On matters of great moral importance, to remain neutral is to fail the test.

Similar moral tests for society arise for each generation. Slavery raised fundamental questions for the British in the early 1800s and in the United States in the Civil War. The movement for the equality of women was a fundamental test beginning in the early 20th century. Segregation had to be rejected in the southern United States in the 1960s and apartheid was the great question in South Africa in the 1980s.

What is the great moral issue of *our* time? For what will we be judged by future generations? Where do our choices most matter?

From among several worthy candidates, I believe our outstanding moral imperative is to maintain the health of the natural systems in which human life is imbedded. Climate change, the destruction of ecosystems, and the extinction of species, for example, constitute a cluster of issues that raise fundamental questions about the way we live. Simply by participating in ordinary life, we affect the viability of the natural systems on which all living creatures depend for their air, water, and food. Undermining these natural systems not only violates moral and aesthetic sensitivities about the well-being of non-human life, but also threatens the well-being of future human communities. If, as seems likely, the ability of the earth's natural systems to support a good quality of life for future generations is degraded, our children and grandchildren will endure great suffering and have legitimate reasons to judge us as failures in the great moral question of our time. On this question, I believe that we are making very good time in exactly the wrong direction.

A Short Personal History

When I finished high school, I had clear plans for my career. I was going to be a scientist, and although I grew up a thousand miles from the nearest ocean, I was interested in marine biology. I enrolled in the honours biochemistry program at the local university.

After a few years, however, I began to realize that science is not just the pursuit of knowledge but also the pursuit of power. I began to realize that power without wisdom is dangerous, and that it is foolish to address the technical question of how fast we are going without also addressing the moral question of which way we are going. In short, I started to ask some of the fundamental questions of ethics.

I began to ask vitally important questions such as:
- What do we value? What is good?
- What is the good life and how do we live it?
- To what life goals should we devote ourselves?
- For what kind of society and world should we be striving?
- How are the goods of society distributed?
- How does scientific research benefit different groups within a society?
- Who should be involved in decisions on these questions?

Eventually, those questions led me to a fundamental shift in my career path. While I never lost my interest and appreciation for scientific research, I became more interested in conversations about ethics and the good life. I had finished the requirements for a bachelor's degree so I decided to take a year off to travel. I spent six months in South America, including three months with a development organization in Guyana, where I lived and worked with people who were profoundly affected by unjust trade and economic relationships. Among my most vivid memories of my time in Guyana was the sight of a forest that had been poisoned by toxic tailings from a bauxite plant. Only bare and dead trunks protruded from the contaminated earth. My first-hand encounters with social and ecological injustices aroused in me a passion for investigating moral and ethical questions – a passion that I had never experienced in the laboratory.

In our society issues of justice and ethics are often treated as matters of personal opinion, and not given much weight beyond that. But I discovered that my church community also regarded these questions as matters of fundamental importance. It is no accident that my interest in ethics went hand in hand with a commitment to a faith community. I care about matters of justice and ethics because my church taught me to care about them.

The Christian Prophetic Tradition

My faith community is part of the Christian tradition, which venerates Jesus of Nazareth as the fullest revelation of the divine. Jesus was a Jewish prophet, healer, and wisdom teacher who challenged the religious and political establishment of Galilee and Judea, then provinces of the Roman Empire. As an alternative to the empire of Caesar, he offered the kingdom of God, in which the will of God would be done on earth. Jesus drew from Jewish law and wisdom and transformed the understanding of how to live in the land. He taught that God's kingdom would be a community of radical equality, unconditional love, non-violent resistance to oppression, and unqualified forgiveness. He was put to death by the representatives of the Roman Empire, but his followers claim that he overcame death and continues to live on in the movement that he began.

Early followers of Jesus tell of how they continued his ministry by teaching and healing in his name, and forming a new kind of community where people shared their possessions, fed the poor, healed the sick, and risked their lives in service to Jesus and one another. This movement was originally referred to as "The Way." The Way was clearly intended to be broadly inclusive, since all good was seen as having the same divine source.

The movement grew slowly over the next three centuries, enduring much persecution; but then, ironically, Emperor Constantine (312–337) adopted this anti-imperial movement and sponsored it as the imperial religion. In doing so, Constantine introduced a tension between the imperial and prophetic streams of the Christian tradition that has been with us ever since. Imperial Christianity became concerned primarily with obedience to authority, life after death, and individual reconciliation with God. The church came to be seen as an institution rather than a popular movement. God came to be seen as a righteous avenger of individual sins rather than the passionate advocate of social justice. Society was assumed to be Christian, and its enemies were identified as demonic. The prophetic focus of Jesus and his earliest followers on a radical alternative to imperial injustices was minimized or abandoned entirely.

Today there remain those who invoke the name of Jesus to justify military conquests, obedience to authority, righteous vengeance, and demonization of enemies. But the prophetic critique of society and the effort to embody God's compassion in concrete institutions and practices has never been completely suppressed.

I am strongly influenced by this tradition of Christian prophetic theology that explores the public importance of our response to God's compassion, justice, and unconditional love. For reasons that will become clear in the progress of this book, I believe this tradition of prophetic faith has an important contribution to make to questions of ecological health.

Pastoral Ministry

Influenced by my growing interest in the ethical questions raised by human powers and my developing conviction that Christian prophetic tradition had something important to say about those questions, I began to explore how I might engage such questions in a vocational way, and eventually engaged in theological study and pastoral ministry.

The ministry has proved to be a vocation with considerable scope. My pastoral work involves close relationships with others, and also allows me to explore spiritual, theological, and ethical questions.

Along with my pastoral work, I pursued two postgraduate degrees in theology and ethics and now share my passion and knowledge with university students by teaching a course called "Living with Respect in Creation: Ecology, Ethics and Theology in Dialogue."

This book emerges from this engagement with both ethics and theology. While those of a different faith or no traditional faith may not share the practices or beliefs of my tradition, I hope they will still find much of value, and will be able to engage even the theological sections of the book with creativity and imagination.

Natural Systems

This book is based on an assumption that healthy natural systems are foundational to any understanding of the good life. By the term "natural systems" I mean local ecosystems – forests, wetlands, grasslands, deserts, and the like – as well as other systems that cycle water, nitrogen, carbon, and other basic elements. People, no less than plants and other animals, live as part of natural systems. Natural systems provide the air we breathe, the water we drink, and the food we eat. Natural systems also absorb many of our waste products. Natural systems are not our "environment" – something outside of us from which we are distinct. Rather they are something of which we are a part, and which are a part of us. People cannot expect to live a good life apart from healthy communities embedded within thriving natural systems.

When natural systems are healthy, we have the best chance of enjoying good health and a good life. When natural systems are unhealthy, when the water and air are polluted or the food contains toxic chemicals, our health is affected in unpredictable ways and our chances of having a good life are dramatically diminished. Healthy natural systems are also important to our emotional, social, and spiritual well-being in ways that are difficult to quantify or predict.

Natural Systems and Social Inequality

To speak of the impacts of pollution and other disruptions of ecosystems on the health of humans in general, however, overlooks their disproportionate impact on vulnerable people in society, such as women, children, and the poor. It is well known that desperation often leads impoverished people to sacrifice long-term sustainability for short-term survival by killing wild (and sometimes endangered) animals for food or cutting down forests for firewood and charcoal. However, more importantly, people with little political or economic power have little ability to protect their environment against exploitation. Companies and governments overlook environmental problems that affect the powerless because the current political and economic systems fail to call those institutions to account.

In the relatively well-off countries in the North, a disproportionate number of garbage and toxic waste disposal facilities are located in close proximity to communities of people of colour, including native communities. The poor areas of larger cities also have higher rates of pollution and corresponding health problems, like asthma.[1] In the impoverished areas of the American Appalachians, whole mountains are removed in search of coal. In my home province of Alberta, the mining of oil sands creates huge lakes of toxic wastes that leach into the Athabasca River upstream of First Nations communities.

In the relatively poorer countries of the South, weaker governments, looser regulations, and greater corruption make it easier for mining and logging companies to extract resources and profits at the expense of the environment and harder for vulnerable people to protect the ecosystems and environmental resources that they depend on.

There are many examples of this. I will never forget hearing a visitor from the South Pacific Islands describe the high rates of birth defects suffered by those whose islands had been used for nuclear tests and the dumping of nuclear wastes. The radiation continues to exact a deadly toll, years later. It is easier for such practices of exploitation to happen where land prices are low, democratic institutions are weak, and officials easily impressed by large companies with deep pockets. The members of the local elite grow wealthier while the poor find their soil and water supplies contaminated. These people are treated as if they do not matter because they are economically and politically powerless. Trends like this have led one Latin American writer to argue that "poverty is the greatest environmental problem of the region."[2]

The study of the interaction of social inequalities and environmental problems is known as social ecology or eco-justice. A related movement that studies the intersection of gender inequalities with ecological problems is known as ecofeminism. This movement has established a profound link between the degradation of "Mother Earth" and social systems that treat women as inferior to men.

An ethic aimed at sustaining the earth systems on which humans depend cannot separate the environment from questions of social and gender equality. In fact, attempting to separate those issues will undermine both. As Pope Benedict XVI wrote in 2007,

> humanity, if it truly desires peace, must be increasingly conscious of the links between natural ecology, or respect for nature, and human ecology. Experience shows that disregard for the environment always harms human coexistence and vice versa."[3]

The Great Turning

How have we so fundamentally misunderstood the human place in relation to the rest of the earth that we undermine the capacity of the earth to sustain us at all? Distorted conceptions of what it means to live a good life have led us astray, and we now have to rethink what we understand the good life to be about and how to live it.

Rethinking, however, is not enough. We need to live more respectfully in our relationship with the rest of creation. Our life practices link with our thinking in complex ways and we need to address both. Thomas Berry calls the development of these new patterns of thinking and living the "Great Work" of our time.[4] Joanna Macy and David Korten call it the "Great Turning."[5]

I make no claim that this book will do anything more than help some of us take a few small steps around the corner. If it does that, however, then I am confident that other sources will help us take additional steps. I offer, then, not a destination, but a direction and a few steps along the way.

I am both a realistic person and a hopeful person. I am realistic because I know that the challenges the human community now faces are serious and not easily solvable. While I am a person of faith, I am not naïve. I do not believe in facing difficult problems with wishful thinking. I do not believe in a God who will supernaturally intervene to rescue us from the difficulties we have created for ourselves. If God were going to prevent great suffering, God would already have done so. That means that it is probable, given current trends, that ecological problems will cause greater and greater suffering. In short, I am not optimistic.

But I am hopeful. I am hopeful because I believe that when people work together they can accomplish what initially seems impossible. I am hopeful because I believe that there is a power for good "creeping through the crannies of the world" like imperceptible rootlets that, in time, penetrate solid rock and split it into pieces.[6] I am hopeful because I believe that those who genuinely desire the best for themselves and future generations will respond to that power and join their efforts to the slow but irresistible pressure for change.

I offer this book in that realistic and hopeful spirit. The challenges facing us are prodigious, and we do not know precisely whether or how they will be overcome. The solutions to our problems are not obvious, and it is important to think carefully about them and to draw on every source of wisdom at our disposal. I believe that God's Spirit is at work in many spheres of human activity – in universities, cooperatives, social movements, religious organizations, businesses, governments, non-governmental organizations, and others – to bring about more just and sustainable communities. I believe that as people share their knowledge, insights, and dreams, and find ways to work together, they will make progress toward ecological sustainability and economic justice. I hope that this book will add some insight from the discipline of theological ethics to the dialogue that is happening.

Overview of the Book

The first chapter of the book explores the complexities of natural systems and why the human systems that manage them often fail. It demonstrates why we should expect instability and err on the side of caution.

The second and third chapters introduce the somewhat abstract topic of ethical theory. The controversy that surrounds the Atlantic seal hunt serves as a case study for exploring three major ethical theories. I propose that a focus on fashioning communities of character more adequately addresses environmental problems than any theory that focuses on individual creatures. Since we learn to be good citizens by engaging in social practices that shape our character, the remainder of this book explores those practices.

Chapters four through eight explore current economic, scientific, and religious practices that need to be reshaped in order to create sustainable communities. Chapter four contrasts traditional and sustainable economics, and describes how the practice of measuring development needs to be refashioned in order to better evaluate the progress of societies. Chapter five contrasts a science-and-technology-based desire to control nature with a more humble approach that is conscious of its inability to fully understand the mystery and complexity of life. Chapter six explores what it would mean to be good stewards of a sacred earth, and the controversial topic of how religious views contribute to environmental problems. Chapter seven describes practices of worship, praise, and lament that treat the rest of creation with reverence. Chapter eight explores how we train ourselves to act hopefully in the midst of fear and danger.

One major theme of the book is the importance of community. Studies of sustainable communities point out the importance of having an intimate connection with surrounding ecosystems. Sustainable communities also have an ethic in which shared social practices train good earth citizens. But the combination of an individualistic culture with globalized economic systems rapidly undermines the ability of communities to protect the natural systems they depend on. This is a problem which will require both careful reflection and the political engagement of citizens on behalf of their communities.

It is my hope that this book will help such engaged citizens to develop the vision and analytic tools necessary to take significant steps towards forming sustainable communities. I hope that readers of this book will feel invited and empowered to participate in becoming a part of this great work of our time.

Chapter One
FRAGILE SYSTEMS

*We are crossing natural thresholds that we cannot see
and violating deadlines that we do not recognize.
Nature is the time keeper, but we cannot see the clock.*

Lester Brown [1]

It happened at a scientific meeting in 1998. A biologist named Joan Kleypas suddenly jumped to her feet and rushed to the toilet to throw up. What made her sick was not an infection or something she had eaten. It was the information being presented.[2]

Kleypas studies calcifiers – marine organisms with shells composed of calcium compounds. Calcifiers include some of the most important and universal organisms in the ocean: mollusks, coral, and many types of plankton. Plankton are the foundation of the ocean food chain, and plankton that photosynthesize produce at least half of the world's oxygen.

The information presented at the meeting revealed that approximately one-third of the carbon dioxide being emitted into our atmosphere is absorbed into ocean water and converted into carbonic acid. Increasing levels of carbon dioxide in the atmosphere (due primarily to the burning of fossil fuels) make ocean water slightly more acidic. Growing acidity has enormous implications for calcifiers because it compromises their ability to make shells. If these organisms, fundamental to life on earth, are in trouble, Kleypas realized, it isn't just the ocean ecosystems that are in trouble – it is all of us. We don't know what levels of acidity these creatures can tolerate, so pumping increasing amounts of carbon dioxide into the atmosphere, as we are doing, is creating a vast uncontrolled experiment with the ocean ecosystem. When the danger of acidification is added to over-fishing, coral bleaching, and climate change, the consequences could be catastrophic.[3] That is what made this pioneering scientist sick to her stomach.

It is dangerous to view natural resources in isolation from the natural systems in which they are embedded. When we do that, we tend to think we can predict the supply of natural resources fairly accurately. But when we view natural resources as parts of natural systems, we have to think more deeply about how they are produced and what happens after we use them.

Farmland is one natural resource vital to feeding a growing population. But what exactly is farmland? A farming magazine once approached several scientists to answer that question, but were unable to find someone who felt competent to do so. The geologists could describe the mineral content, the entomologists the insect life, the microbiologists the bacterial life, and so on, but no one could do it all, and even all of them together couldn't begin to describe all the complex interactions between the minerals, plants, fungi, and insects.[4]

Land then, is a natural system in which many components interact with each other. In addition to fertile soil (itself a complex system of minerals, decomposing organic matter, water, microorganisms, fungi, and insects), productive land must have adequate sunlight, access to the right mix of gases in the atmosphere, and the right amount of uncontaminated water. Further, in order to be productive it must escape being eroded, flooded, overgrazed, trampled, paved, or otherwise built over.

What is true of land is also true of water and air: fresh water is part of the hydrological cycle, and air is part of the atmosphere, both of which are complex systems that we only partially understand. And because all natural resources are embedded in these imperfectly understood natural systems, we vastly oversimplify the reality when we treat natural resources only as commodities.

The Complexity of Natural Systems

When the science of ecology was developed in the late 19th century, scientists proposed that individual species were related to their environment like organs are related to a human body.[5] Sometimes called an organic view, this early understanding of ecology expected communities of plants and animals to develop into mature states of biodiversity characterized by balance, harmony, and long-term stability. A natural community could then be assessed as to whether it was young or mature, healthy or diseased, similar to the way a doctor assesses the human body. Ecologists could then diagnose problems and suggest treatments to restore a natural community to balance and keep it healthy.

This organic model was discarded after Arthur Tansley proposed the concept of the ecosystem in 1935. While the organic view focused on the interactions of plant and animal organisms, the ecosystem view recognized that soil, nutrients, and climate interact with those organisms in complex ways. Ecosystems traced the flow of energy and nutrients through food chains.

Scientists also identified positive and negative feedback loops within ecosystems. Negative feedback loops tend to keep ecosystems stable. For example, if a large number of rabbits survive a warm winter, they may consume all the food resources in the area, causing a significant number of them to starve. The availability of food resources is a negative feedback loop that keeps rabbit populations in check. More rabbits mean that foxes and other predators will also be well-fed and reproduce more effectively. But if there get to be too many predators, then the number of rabbits will fall, and many of the predators will starve. Thus the relationship of prey and predator functions as a negative feedback loop to keep the populations of each in balance.

The ecosystem model expects a normally functioning ecosystem to be stable and balanced. But more recent research has revealed that while negative feedback loops may keep ecosystems stable in the short term, ecosystems often make very dramatic and sudden shifts over longer periods. This revolutionized the study of ecology. Ecosystems, even in the absence of human interference, are now considered to be dynamic and unpredictable.

This dynamism happens partly because of positive feedback loops, created when a small change in one aspect of the ecosystem triggers a change in another part that reinforces the first change. For example, a lack of rainfall leads water tables to fall and soil to dry out. Plants and trees then reduce their metabolic rates and produce less water vapour, which leads to lower rates of rainfall and a self-reinforcing spiral of drought. Eventually, however, it will rain, moisture levels in the soil will rise, and puddles, ponds, and streams will fill. The evaporation from those sources, combined with increased respiration from vegetation, will increase the humidity in the atmosphere and contribute to more rainfall. Thus, positive feedback loops can contribute to alternating cycles of drought and rainfall.

Threshold Effects

The instability of ecosystems is also due to threshold effects, tipping points, or non-linear events, where gradual changes may suddenly trigger dramatic shifts, just like the proverbial straw that broke the camel's back. Outside my window, for example, snow and ice accumulated for months in below zero temperatures. But in early April, the temperature finally rose enough to exceed the melting point and everything started to thaw. The freezing/melting point of water is a threshold or tipping point at which dramatic changes happen with startling rapidity. So is the boiling point.[6] However, systems may be relatively stable on either side of the tipping point, just as water below the freezing point stays frozen.

Natural systems are complex networks of systems and communities of communities. A slight variation in any one part of the network – water or soil chemistry, light and atmospheric conditions, evolving insect plant and animal species – may have a profound impact on the whole. Because systems overlap and interconnect, small changes may accumulate throughout the network. Everything might appear normal until an unseen and unexpected threshold is crossed, and the behaviour of the entire system suddenly shifts to a radically new mode.

For over a century, the Atlantic cod harvest produced an average catch of approximately 250,000 tons per year. But with the introduction of factory trawlers, and without effective international regulation, the harvest peaked at 800,000 tons in 1968. By the mid-1970s, however, the catch had crashed to less than 150,000 tons. After Canada and the United States extended their offshore jurisdiction in 1976 and enforced scientifically determined quotas, the catch increased to about 250,000 tons and remained relatively stable for a decade, until it suddenly crashed again in 1992 and the fishery was closed.[7] Some scientists had warned that quotas were too high, but few expected the dramatic declines that occurred. The reasons for the crash are still not clear, but what is clear is that some threshold was crossed that drastically reduced the number of cod to the point that the fishery has still not recovered twenty years later.

There are a number of other thresholds that are of concern to scientists. Forests and wetlands purify air and water, produce oxygen, prevent erosion, play important roles in flood prevention, and serve as habitat for countless species. The effects of converting more than half of the world's forests and wetlands to agriculture and urbanization are unknown. The loss of these habitats also threatens an estimated 12% of birds, 25% of mammals, and 32% of amphibians.[8] The impact of losing large numbers of species has been compared to knocking rivets out of an aircraft.[9] The point at which the aircraft fails due to lost rivets is unknown.

A few degrees of global warming may have threshold effects that accelerate the effects of climate change. The loss of polar ice, the accelerating melting rate of glaciers, the changing ocean circulation patterns, the melting of permafrost, and the decimation of boreal forest could all produce threshold effects that would result in a very different world than the one in which we now live.

By their very nature, threshold events are difficult to study, and it may only be possible to identify a tipping point in hindsight. But the possibility that one might occur is worth considering, and when there is a reasonable possibility that such a tipping point might dramatically change the environments on which we rely, it is prudent to take concrete action to avoid that.

Human Systems

Human systems are as complex as natural and ecological systems and equally vulnerable to failure. Corporations, governments, and universities are the easiest human systems to define, but more abstract entities like social, economic, and cultural systems are also important.

Human systems fail for all kinds of reasons: goals may be misguided, individuals in key roles in the system may be corrupt or incompetent, the system may be too rigid to respond to new stresses or too flexible to maintain integrity under stress.

Such failures have been described in theological terms as due to either finitude, sin, or a combination of the two. Human systems are finite because we do not and cannot know everything, and our systems cannot take everything into account. The failure of the regulatory system for managing the Atlantic fishery, for example, was in part due to the finite abilities of scientists to collectively understand all of the factors affecting cod habitat and population dynamics.

While finitude is an unavoidable part of being human, sin is a rebellion against our human nature. The failure to recognize that finitude is part of our human condition leads us to assume that our knowledge is complete, or that the limited goals of a company, nation, or group are universal. Humans and human systems act sinfully when, in the pursuit of their own limited goals, they produce ends that are unjust for others. For example, corporations whose interests lie in producing or consuming fossil fuels seek out scientists who deny the majority scientific opinion on climate change in order to justify their continuing exploitation of the resource.

There is no sin in having a difference of opinion. The sin lies in being so focused on our own narrow short-term interest that we ignore credible risks with negative consequences for others because taking action on them would hurt our interest.

Individuals and systems, of course, do not always act according to their narrow self-interest. Individuals, organizations, and corporations involved in the fishery have a long-term interest in preserving the fish stock, and some of them acted against their own narrow self-interest in calling for a reduction in fishing quotas. We all have a long-term interest in climate stability. Individuals and systems are sinful when they sacrifice the public good to narrow short-term interests.

The finitude and sinfulness of humans and their systems means that systems will often fail. No system is perfect, but some systems are still better than others, and systems that plan for human finitude and sinfulness are more effective than those that expect perfection.

The Tragedy of the Commons

In a famous article, Garrett Hardin imagines a pasture open to all who want to make use of it. Hardin argues that each herdsman will try to keep as many cattle as possible on the commons, even when the pasture is being overgrazed, because individual herdsmen will receive the full benefit of additional animals but the cost of overgrazing will be shared among all who use the pasture. Each herdsman, acting individually and in his own self-interest, will conclude that the only sensible choice is to keep increasing his herd. This creates what Hardin called "the tragedy of the commons," for eventually the pasture is completely overgrazed and the community collapses.

Hardin pointed out that the tragedy of the commons applies to many of our environmental problems: disappearing forests, expanding deserts, falling water tables, collapsing fisheries, rising temperatures, and increasing populations. Individuals and groups acting separately in the pursuit of their own interests often destroy the natural systems that are vital to their well-being. At a small scale, dog walkers in a local park will spoil the park for everyone by failing to pick up their dog droppings. At a much larger scale, individual nations, acting in the absence of international agreements, continually increase their greenhouse gas emissions because they fear that cutting back would jeopardize their economic well-being. This creates the tragedy.

Hardin concluded, "Each man is locked into a system that compels him to increase his herd without limit – in a world that is limited. Ruin is the destination toward which all men rush, each pursuing his own best interest in a society that believes in the freedom of the commons. Freedom in a commons brings ruin to all." [10]

The only alternative to the tragedy of the commons, Hardin argued, is some system of "mutual coercion, mutually agreed upon" in which the interested parties are able to deliberate together about the health of the commons and agree on mutually binding limits. In other words, they have to stop acting as isolated individuals, companies, or nations and begin acting as a community (or a community of nations).

The tragedy of the commons scenario also suggests that societies that stress individual freedom will likely be fragile ecologically, and an international community in which national sovereignty is not balanced by international institutions will be unsustainable.

One possible response to the tragedy of the commons is to privatize natural systems, under the assumption that the owners of private property will act to protect their properties from over-exploitation. However, many natural systems cannot be owned privately. Fish, birds, and other animals migrate across national borders and past offshore limits. Many lakes and forests are simply too large for any one individual, or even corporation, to own privately. An owner of a natural resource (a river, for example) would have dictatorial power over those who need the resource. Forests and rangelands often stretch across national borders and the oceans and the atmosphere are international.[11] Private owners are not always knowledgeable, competent, or responsible enough to exercise effective stewardship over the natural systems that they own, and their failures often have significant impact on others who rely on their property. And a "tragedy of fragmentation" happens when a landscape is fragmented among multiple owners, making it harder to develop an overall plan.[12]

Common Property Regimes

Fortunately there is an alternative to both private property and the kind of free-for-all that Hardin imagines. There are many examples of fragile natural systems that are successfully managed by using a form of common ownership and collective management, usually referred to as Common Property Regimes (CPRs). Some institutions have intensively used and successfully managed pastures, water systems, fisheries, and other natural systems for hundreds of years.[13]

Some of the most important principles for successful management of common property are that:[14]

- the natural system is important enough to those who use it that they are willing to invest time and energy to monitor and protect it;
- the natural system is used and managed by people who live in close proximity with the system and can monitor it closely (the larger the system, the more difficult this is, so smaller systems are more effectively managed);
- the institution is effective in involving all the users of the resource in decision-making and has their trust in solving conflicts;
- the institution has a variety of sanctions available to encourage compliance and discourage abuse of the resource;
- the users/managers of the system are able to control the resource and protect it from those who are not part of the management system;
- the management system is supported by regulatory and legal systems at all relevant levels of government.

These principles suggest two important implications for the management and protection of natural systems. First, the importance of systems being managed by people who live intimately with them is consistent with the ethical principle of *subsidiarity,* which suggests that power should be vested at the smallest, most local, and least complex competent level of authority. Governments and other organizations at higher levels of complexity should be subsidiary to local authorities and support rather than undermine the smaller, more local institutions. This does not mean, however, that governments are unimportant. Government regulation plays a vital role in maintaining the integrity of natural systems. International institutions are also important for dealing with international problems. The principle of subsidiarity means that we must design the bodies responsible for managing natural systems at an appropriate scale.

Secondly, because natural systems overlap and inter-relate, the human systems that manage and protect them will also need to overlap and interrelate. Just as a forest in a mountainous region may overlap several different watersheds, so the management systems for each will have to relate to others. The need for overlapping systems and the principle of subsidiarity imply a preference for a federal system of government, in which many levels of political organization cooperate and work closely with non-governmental organizations to protect and manage natural systems.

Human systems, like natural systems, are fragile, and the interaction between fragile human systems and fragile natural systems makes everything more fragile. A failure in a human system could be catastrophic for an ecosystem, and that in turn could cause serious social and economic problems for human communities.

Pope Benedict XVI writes:

Alongside the ecology of nature there exists what can be called a "human" ecology, which in turn demands a "social" ecology. All this means that humanity, if it truly desires peace, must be increasingly conscious of the links between natural ecology, or respect for nature, and human ecology. Experience shows that disregard for the environment always harms human coexistence and vice versa.[15]

Barry Lopez makes the point more dramatically: "a politics with no biology, or a politics without field biology... is a vision of the gates of Hell."[16]

Planning for a Wreck

The fragility of ecosystems, human finitude and sinfulness, the fallibility of organizations, and the dangers of social collapse and state failure are all sobering reminders that we cannot gamble with the natural systems on which we depend. There are limits to how much we can extract from natural systems, and we often do not know what those limits are.

Managing a renewable resource for economic benefit, commented one scientist, is as difficult as "balancing a marble on top of a dome."[17] Sustainable yield may itself be an unsustainable idea, according to some scientists who have studied the collapse of fisheries, because "science is probably incapable of predicting safe levels of resource exploitation." [18] While there is no scientific certainty about sustainable yields, science is able to reduce the level of uncertainty. In other words, knowing that fisheries are in fact variable and that there will be good years and bad years, and knowing that scientific predictions and systems are themselves fallible, fisheries should be managed so that enough fish are left even given a bad prediction in a bad year. The same approach can be applied to many other natural systems.

The realization that ecosystems are not inherently balanced and stable implies that we have to be far more cautious about our ability to understand and predict both what natural systems can produce, and how much waste they can afford. We are embedded in natural systems and cannot escape them (even if we wanted to), so we cannot avoid establishing systems to manage them. But we must err on the side of caution and prudence and focus on long-term resilience rather than short-term efficiency.[19] In other words, we must relearn the old farmer's advice to "plan for a wreck." To plan for a wreck means to expect the unexpected, to plan with large margins of error, to leave allowances for lower than expected crop yields, higher than expected input costs, and the occasional car wreck. If we plan for the worst case scenario, then the worst we can do is meet our expectations. But it is more likely that we will end up with a surplus.

For decades in North America, the political winds have varied between *laissez-faire* economics and the effort to develop strong regulatory mechanisms to manage natural systems. Economist Kenneth Boulding once described the two approaches as cowboy economics and spaceship earth. The first approach implies we can let market systems ride roughshod over natural systems without significant concern.[20] The other approach sees Earth as a giant spaceship with every system under complete human management. Such total management – in light of the complexity and fragility of natural systems – is a project of such gigantic hubris as to be laughable. As the failure of Apollo 13 so clearly demonstrated, an unexpected glitch can put all the passengers in mortal peril. We cannot afford to operate our planetary home on such fine tolerances.

Larry Rasmussen suggests we should be thinking of daycare earth. Daycare centres are designed for toddlers who will not be managed and will trip over every bump in the rug. Responsible daycare providers err on the side of caution and try to eliminate every hazard. In the same way, we need to err on the side of caution with respect to the natural systems in which we live and on which we depend.[21]

Our modern economic and political systems do not excel at caution, however. Modern political systems emphasize individual freedom, limited only when such freedom infringes on the freedom of our neighbours.

Economic systems emphasize our freedom as consumers to choose what we want to buy and as producers to produce whatever will make a profit, limited only by those regulations considered necessary to protect public health and safety. Powerful political forces, especially in the United States, but also in other Western democracies, are suspicious of any restrictions on individual liberty.[22]

But as we have seen, many individuals acting freely in pursuit of their own interests will often bring ruin to the fragile natural systems on which we all depend. This means that societies will often have to choose between individual freedoms and healthy ecosystems.

Such choices raise all kinds of difficult political questions. The findings of this chapter suggest that individual freedom will often have to be curtailed in order to preserve natural systems on which many depend for life. If we continue to emphasize freedom, are we choosing liberty over life itself? And if we decide for freedom, and our choice undermines natural systems on which many people depend, is it fair for us to make that choice for them? Is it fair that we in our generation make that choice for future generations? Whose life are we talking about? Is it only human life that matters? What value should be placed on the lives of individual creatures, species, and ecosystems?

Chapter Two
WE ANIMALS AND OUR ETHICS

O God, enlarge within us the sense of fellowship
with all living things, our brothers the animals
to whom thou gavest the earth as their home in
  common with us.
May we realize that they live not for us alone
but for themselves and for thee,
and that they love the sweetness of life.

Saint Basil the Great[1] (330–379 CE)

The questions with which I closed the last chapter are questions of ethics – questions about what is right and good and fair, about what makes for a good life. Exploring the field of ethics can help us learn to live a life that is good for individuals, communities, other creatures, and the natural systems of which we are a part.

Ethics is the study of the various views of the good life. We are all constantly involved in ethical choices about what life is for and what is important. Sometimes we are aware of those choices, but more often we make them unconsciously. In choosing a career and following it, for example, we make conscious ethical choices about the relative importance of financial reward, social status, education, and making a social contribution. Likewise, the way we live in natural systems involves often unconscious ethical choices that need to be brought into consciousness so that they can be examined more carefully.

Although our society tends to see ethics as a matter of private and personal choice, people who share a common profession, such as lawyers, find it impossible to work together without agreement on certain fundamental ethical commitments. An unethical lawyer undermines the whole practice of law. So professional groups usually have ethical codes that set out what is expected of members of the profession and means of discipline when those expectations are breached. Similarly, nations must find agreement on some ethical questions by making laws. Ethical codes and laws restrict personal choices for the sake of the good of the wider community. There is a constant balance and negotiation between individual freedom and the social necessity to work within communally-agreed limits.

As we seek to live responsibly within complex and overlapping systems, our ethics must also consider what is good for the natural systems within which humans live. In the recent past, many of the most controversial ethical questions have involved human relationships to other animals.

The Atlantic Seal Hunt and Ethical Controversy

In late February and early March, female harp seals gather in large groups on ice floes in the Gulf of St. Lawrence and off the coast of Newfoundland and Labrador to give birth to their pups, which are born with beautiful white fur coats. For the first 12–14 days, the whitecoats are nursed by their mothers, building up a thick layer of fat. At that point the mothers return to the sea to breed, leaving the pups alone on the ice. Shortly after the mothers leave, the pups lose their white fur and turn a steely grey. For the next few weeks these "beaters" survive off their fat layer while they grow and gain strength. At the age of three months, the beaters are able to leave the ice permanently and survive in the open ocean.[2]

During the three-month period when the seal pups are on the ice, seal hunters travel in ships through dangerous shifting ice to the whelping grounds, where they work quickly to harvest as many of the vulnerable young pups as possible within the constraints of quotas and a short sealing season. Some seals are shot, but most have their skulls crushed by a club before being skinned. At one time the seal's oil rich layer of fat was valuable, but now only the pelts are collected and the rest of the carcass is left on the ice.

In the 1960s, some witnesses to the hunt claimed that hunting baby seals was cruel and morally wrong and began to organize protests and boycotts. They were supported by animal welfare groups in Europe, the United States, and Canada. The protests led the European Economic Union to ban imports of the whitecoat pelts in 1983. In 1987, the Canadian government established regulations to ensure that the seals were killed humanely. It also banned the hunt of whitecoats.

The hunters, supported by the Canadian government's Department of Fisheries and Oceans, defend the practice as an important part of the culture and economy of Atlantic Canada. The critics respond that a cruel practice is wrong in spite of custom or economic need. The hunters deny that the hunt is cruel and argue that the seal hunt is at least as humane as the way cattle are slaughtered by the meatpacking industry. The critics claim that in the competition to get their share of the quota, the hunters often don't confirm that the seal is dead before skinning it. They have released video showing seals moving while being skinned. The hunters respond that even a clearly dead seal will sometimes move because of a "swimming reflex." The critics argue that the hunt is decimating the seal population of the North Atlantic. Hunters claim that the Canadian government scientifically manages the hunt and although seal populations fluctuate, their populations are healthy. They also claim that without the hunt, seal populations would grow and decimate already vulnerable populations of cod and other fish. The critics point out that the cod fishery was also scientifically managed right up to the point at which cod stocks declined catastrophically in the late 1980s. And so the debate goes on, with claim and counter-claim.

How might a dispute like this be solved? Is the seal hunt wrong? And if so, what is wrong about it? The answers to those questions are not just of concern to those involved in the Atlantic seal hunt. For if the treatment of animals is a moral issue, then the ways in which farm animals are raised, transported, and slaughtered is also open for scrutiny.

Sometimes in ethical controversies there are factual claims that can be investigated and either confirmed or disproved. For example, veterinary scientists have investigated the accusation that seals are sometimes skinned alive, and found that 98 percent of the seals are killed humanely.[3] Animal welfare groups dispute that study and quote other studies.

Even if that finding were accepted, however, it still means that two percent of seals are not killed humanely. Is that an acceptable level of suffering? And how do you define "humane" killing? Those are ethical questions that cannot be resolved by scientific investigation alone.

The Treatment of Non-Human Animals: Three Ethical Theories

These questions lead rather quickly to a more abstract set of questions: What makes something good or bad, right or wrong, cruel or humane? Those questions belong to the field of ethical theory. In this chapter, I will describe attempts to address ethical questions about the treatment of non-human animals using three major theories of philosophical ethics.[4] In the next chapter I will examine how one of these theories has been adapted to meet the challenges of our postmodern world.

Humans are, of course, animals, and to be technically correct I should always say non-human animals when I don't mean to include humans. For reasons of style and brevity, however, I often use the term animals in the narrower sense, and I trust the reader will follow my meaning.

1. Natural Law

The original ethical theory is the tradition of natural law. This view suggests there is a law of nature that defines the goal or purpose of each thing. The Greek scientist and philosopher Aristotle (384–322 BCE), who first carefully articulated a natural law ethic, integrated his understandings of science and ethics. He believed that careful study of an object could establish its characteristic purpose, function, or goal. Establishing an object's purpose leads to an understanding of what it makes it good at accomplishing that purpose. So, for example, if the purpose of a watch is to keep time (rather than to impress the neighbours), then a good watch will keep accurate time.[5]

According to Aristotle, living beings also have a purpose, and good, healthy creatures accomplish that purpose with excellence. A healthy plant grows luxuriously. A healthy animal grows and is also able to interact with its surroundings energetically. Humans add the ability to think and reason to the qualities they have in common with plants and animals. A good person is therefore one who is able to do the activities of life in a reasonable way. Only a human can reason about how to respond to danger – animals react by either fighting or fleeing. The reasonable way to respond to danger is usually referred to as courage, which is the "golden mean" between the extremes of being either rash or cowardly.[6]

Courage is an example of a virtue, which simply means a good habit. A person cannot decide to be courageous on the spur of the moment. It is a basic and enduring disposition that some people have and others don't. While most modern accounts of ethics focus on individual decisions, Aristotle's account of ethics emphasizes the enduring qualities of character, the way we think, perceive, and behave. For a human being to really flourish and live a good life, he or she must develop these virtuous qualities of character. These virtuous qualities are the human purpose; they are what make human life good. The Greek word for purpose or function is *telos*, and so ethical theories based on natural purpose are called teleological.

In the thirteenth century, the Catholic theologian Thomas Aquinas integrated Aristotle's natural law into Christian theology. He taught that there is a divine plan that operates in nature, that the natural order can therefore be equated with the moral order, and that scientific and theological data should reinforce each other in revealing the moral good. He added three "theological virtues": faith, hope, and love. The natural law perspectives of Aristotle and Aquinas profoundly influenced Western theology, ethics, and law.

Natural law has been used to deny any human obligation to animals or the natural world. My summary of that argument goes as follows:

Plants exist to provide food for animals, and animals exist to provide food for humans. We have moral obligations to humans because they are rational creatures made in God's image. Animals are fundamentally different, and we have no ethical obligations to them. Our treatment of them is morally relevant only to the extent that it affects other people.

People holding this view would say that the seal hunt is fine as long as it is beneficial to humans.

Other proponents of natural law acknowledge that although animals cannot reason or communicate like humans, they can feel pain like humans, and inflicting pain violates the natural rights of animals. On this basis, people with this view oppose vivisection and other common forms of cruelty to animals.

Still other natural law theorists oppose cruelty to animals because of the impact on people, rather than because of any moral obligation to animals. They believe animal cruelty reinforces cruel tendencies in the person inflicting the cruelty, making them callous and insensitive to human suffering.

The modern environmental movement sometimes assumes an implicit natural law. Earlier theories of ecology that assumed well-ordered and stable ecosystems led many environmentalists to defend an undisturbed nature. They argue that ecological problems only arise when humans interfere with the natural order and that we are morally obligated to preserve at least some wilderness in its "unspoiled state."

Natural law has some value to ecological ethics because it takes nature and science into account as partners in ethical consideration. In order to decide whether a practice is cruel or not, we need some understanding of the characteristic way of life of other creatures and what it means for them to flourish, whether it is in a zoo, a barn, or a wild state.

To say that a practice is cruel, however, is not just a claim about what is good for animals. It is also a claim about what is good for people. Opposition to cruelty to animals is a moral claim that humans should be compassionate and concerned for the well-being of animals. So moral claims about cruelty cannot be based solely on scientific observations of animals but must include an understanding of why a good person should care about the well-being of animals.

Problems with Natural Law

There are a number of problems with natural law. First, the link between the moral and natural orders is no longer widely accepted. While pre-modern people might have seen an earthquake as a sign of divine punishment, for example, those instructed in plate tectonics would see it as a consequence of geological forces. An ethic focused on natural law also equates nature (the world as it is) with creation (the world as God intended it to be).[7] This equation has been seriously critiqued by theologians who argue that God's original intention for the world has been frustrated by human sin.

Second, natural law theory depends on a view of nature's design that has been strongly challenged by evolutionary theory. While Aristotle might have described the purpose of a giraffe's long neck as helping it to reach food in tall trees, the theory of natural selection suggests that giraffe ancestors with progressively longer necks thrived because they were able to reach food other animals could not.[8] An animal's nature is therefore seen as the result of thousands of generations of natural selection rather than a given purpose.

Subsequently, while it is obvious that a tool (like a hammer) has a purpose or function, to the modern mind it is not clear that living beings have one. Animals and plants, for example, may have a niche in an ecosystem, but not a natural purpose. It is even less clear that humans have an obvious function or purpose.

Third, as we have seen, the idea that ecosystems are characterized by regular and stable processes that can yield a law of nature has been strongly challenged by a much more dynamic view of natural systems.

Finally, different cultures have different perspectives on what is "natural." There is no easy correspondence between observable facts and the meanings that different cultures apply to them. It is often impossible even to describe the "facts" in the absence of some cultural assumptions. Aboriginal hunters and European vegetarians, for example, have very different perspectives on what happens when an animal dies. As a result they also differ on whether some hunting practices are cruel.

Natural law theory flourished over many centuries, and made important contributions to the development of moral theory, international law, and human rights. But because of the differing cultural assumptions about what is natural, pluralistic societies find it difficult to agree on any one version of natural law. Each religious and cultural tradition has a different view and efforts to reach agreement prove extremely difficult. Societies that are dominated by one religious or moral tradition find it much easier to accept traditions of natural law. Such societies became much less common in the Western world following the Reformation of the sixteenth century. But natural law theory remains common in Roman Catholic moral theology and some other contexts.

2. Utilitarian Ethics and Animal Liberation
Animal Liberation

Since the 1970s, philosopher Peter Singer has argued that our exclusion of non-human animals from moral concern is similar to exclusions of women and blacks, and that there needs to be a movement of animal liberation. Singer coined the term *speciesism* to criticize the failure to take the interests of animals into account. Singer argues that an animal that is capable of suffering and enjoyment has interests, and ethics should respect those interests as much as it does the interests of humans. A being that can suffer has *sentience*, and sentient beings have interests.

He proposes that the line between sentient and non-sentient beings be placed somewhere between an oyster and a shrimp. Presumably it would be acceptable to put a worm on a fish hook because a worm is not sentient, but not to use the hook to catch a fish because a fish *is* sentient. Singer believes that we have a moral obligation to respect the interests of all sentient beings equally.

Singer is particularly critical of the ways in which animals are treated in scientific experimentation and agriculture. He thinks that intensive livestock farms where animals are confined to small pens and have very limited mobility are morally problematic. He proposes that respecting the interests of animals requires radical changes in our practices of eating, farming, scientific research, hunting, and trapping. He also opposes wearing products derived from animals and the use of animals in circuses, zoos, and rodeos.

Only individuals can suffer, so Singer is not concerned about the possibility of species extinction or the destruction of ecosystems. He would oppose the seal hunt because it disregards the interests of individual seals. He would be particularly disturbed by the suffering inflicted on seals, but would not be concerned about the impacts of the hunt on the overall survival of the species or on the marine ecosystem.

Utilitarianism
Singer's concern for animals is based on an ethical theory that focuses on the consequences of actions. According to this theory, called utilitarianism or consequentialism, actions are not good or bad in themselves but are judged in terms of their utility or usefulness in contributing to

good consequences. Good actions are those that produce the highest possible quantity of good and the least amount of harm. So, for example, telling a lie is usually wrong because the lie hurts the person lied to. But if the lie were told to protect an innocent person hiding from a murderous intruder, the amount of pain caused by the lie would be small compared to the consequences of telling the truth.

Utilitarian theory inevitably leads to attempts to quantify and calculate how much good is produced by an action (does the lie produce more good than bad?). It also seems familiar to many because the emphasis on quantifying appeals to our modern interest in calculation and measurement. Economic analysis, for example, often implicitly assumes a utilitarian theory of ethics: If an economic analysis shows that the benefits outweigh the costs, the presumption goes, it must be the right thing to do. These calculations often acquire an appearance of scientific objectivity. But this scientific veneer obscures a number of difficulties with the focus on consequences.

The first difficulty is determining what form of good result should be pursued. Utilitarians distinguish between an intrinsic good, which is valued for its own sake, and an instrumental good, which is a means to an end. Jeremy Bentham (1748–1832) argued that the experience of pleasure and (and the absence of pain) should be seen as the intrinsic good. He argued that since animals have the ability to suffer and feel pleasure, their well-being should be included in calculations of the consequences of an action.

John Stuart Mill (1806–1873) argued that happiness was the highest good, but that there were different grades of happiness, and only truly noble people were able to fully know true happiness. A decadent person might know sensual pleasures, for example, but would miss the fully human happiness of artistic expression or public service. Mill famously wrote, "It is better to be a human being dissatisfied than a pig satisfied; better to be Socrates dissatisfied than a fool satisfied."[9] Such understandings of the good not only put human happiness on a completely different level than animal pleasures, but also make calculations almost impossible.

All creatures share basic needs such as food, clean water, and freedom from severe physical pain. Chickens in an intensive livestock operation have their basic needs met but are confined to small metal cages stacked in layers. Such chickens would be happier in a free-range facility. Is the freedom to move a peripheral interest or a basic need? And how should that interest be measured in relation to the basic human need for food? The challenges of assessing these diverse and competing interests are enormous.

It is much easier to quantify and calculate instrumental goods than intrinsic ones. Money, for example, is a means to an end, an instrumental good. It is much easier to quantify than happiness, so cost-benefit analyses and calculations of economic exchanges routinely use money to predict consequences. Such calculations have the appearance of scientific objectivity, but obscure the fact that what is being calculated is only an instrumental good. Focusing on easily measurable instrumental goods however, may undermine intrinsic ones. Money is easy to count, but as Ebenezer Scrooge discovered, the effort to become rich can interfere with the pursuit of an intrinsic good like friendship.

Singer acknowledges the difficulties in measuring and comparing different kinds of pain and pleasure and thus limits his focus to the prevention of severe suffering.

This limitation, however, also restricts the ability of this theory to give concrete guidance in other situations.

A second problem with utilitarian ethics is that it asks us to predict the consequences of any particular course of action. Consequences, however, are notoriously difficult to predict. Even the wisest person can overlook important outcomes of an action, especially in dealing with natural systems, which are so poorly understood.

Thirdly, there are times when an act is wrong in principle even when the overall consequences are good. Since the terrorist attacks of September 11, 2001, for example, torture has been practiced and defended as a means of getting information on potential acts of terror (although information gained under torture is notoriously unreliable). But torture is a violation of international law and human rights codes because it is widely viewed as intrinsically wrong. In the same way, skinning a seal alive should be seen as intrinsically wrong, even if the overall consequences of such an act are positive. There are times when the ends do not justify the means.

Singer's utilitarian appeal to minimize the suffering of animals is at its most persuasive in bringing to consciousness the cruelty casually inflicted on animals in certain scientific and agricultural practices. But his argument is undercut by how a focus on consequences allows for a good end to excuse cruel means.

3. Deontological Ethics and Animal Rights

In 1983, philosopher Tom Regan proposed that human rights should be extended to animals.[10] In doing so, he drew on a theory of ethics that dates back to the German philosopher Immanuel Kant (1724–1804). Kant proposed that rational people should base their actions on a principle that all other rational persons could recognize as reasonable. He called this universal rational principle the categorical imperative – *categorical* because it is unconditional and unqualified; *imperative* because it establishes a moral obligation. Kant's categorical imperative is that we should always act so as to treat ourselves and other individuals as an end, and never only as a means to an end.

Kant makes a fundamental distinction between moral subjects and moral objects. Humans are capable of making choices and acting with conscious intent and are therefore moral subjects. Moral subjects have inherent value (value in themselves), while moral objects have only instrumental value (a value as a means to accomplish some other end). We have the duty to treat people with the respect due to them as subjects with inherent value. Subjects with inherent value have rights to equality, liberty, happiness, life, and property. In this way, this theory of ethics (called *deontology* from the Greek word for "duty") establishes both inalienable rights that are inherent to all moral subjects, and duties that all moral people are obligated to observe.

In everyday life, we often treat other people as means to ends, but the categorical imperative requires that we never treat them *only* as means (objects). If I hire a taxi driver to drive me across town, paying the cab driver acknowledges him as a subject although I am treating him or her as a means to the end of getting across town.

Some scholars have suggested that deontological theory has important implications for environmental ethics because people have a right to a safe, healthy, and livable environment. Deontology has difficulty, however, accounting for our obligations to children, the mentally disabled, the mentally ill, animals, and other living creatures not considered competent to act as subjects. This may lead to the assumption that it is permissible to treat such beings only as means to ends.

Tom Regan rejected the idea that only moral subjects have inherent value and argued that any creature that is a "subject-of-a-life" has inherent value. To be a subject-of-a-life, an animal must have a sense of itself, be able to remember past experiences and anticipate future ones, and have a sense of its own welfare so that it can take action to protect itself from danger and advance its well-being. Regan believes that most mammals meet these criteria and should be considered as having inherent value. They therefore have a right to be treated with the same respect as all other individuals with inherent value.

Among other things, this leads Regan to propose that humans should not eat mammals, that animal farming and experimentation on animals should be ended, and that any use of animals for entertainment or sport (as in zoos, rodeos, and bullfights) is unjust. With regard to the seal hunt, there is no doubt that Regan would view seals as subjects-of-a-life with inherent value, and therefore with the right to life and security. He would not be concerned with the impact of the hunt on the species or ecosystem, but only with the interference with the rights of individual animals.

There are a number of problems with Regan's proposal to extend rights to animals. One problem is that it assigns the same level of rights to all animals that have rights (including humans). This would create an enormous number of rights conflicts. What should a farmer do when a pack of coyotes attacks a domestic dog? Does a rat have the same rights as the child it might bite?

Another problem is that the animal rights perspective derives its vision of moral standing from human rights. The animals that deserve rights are mammals like us. Many biologists, however, point out that there are many plants, fish, insects, and invertebrates that are essential to ecosystems. Should there not be ethical consideration for them? The theory of animal rights establishes a firm line. Those on one side of the line have rights and we have a duty to respect those rights. Those on the other side have no rights and we have no duties to them. Can they be treated as mere means to human ends? By defining some animals as subject-of-a-life and only assigning rights to them, Regan effectively denies any moral consideration to all other living things.

Individualism

Animal rights and animal liberation share a serious flaw. They focus exclusively on individuals and fail to take species or ecosystems into account. Only an individual can have interests, feel pleasure or pain, or be a subject-of-a-life. Neither Regan nor Singer is interested in the extinction of species or the health of ecosystems. Regan even uses the term "environmental fascism" to refer to the subordination of the rights of individual animals to concerns for species and ecosystems. He argues that if we respect the rights of the individuals that make up a biotic community, the community itself will be preserved.

But most of those responsible for managing national parks and wildlife populations disagree. They point out that ecosystems are incredibly dynamic, and that giving special ethical standing to individual animals threatens the balance and equilibrium of the ecosystem.

Individuals, though, whether human or animal, are always parts of greater wholes, and it is often hard to distinguish the good of the individual from that of the species or ecosystem. Consider salmon. At the height of their strength and power, salmon return from the ocean and fight their way back upstream in order to spawn. Once they spawn, they die. If the good of the salmon is conceived in terms of individual well-being, it is hard to understand how spawning (and consequent death) can be seen as good for the salmon. But it makes absolutely no biological sense to speak of the good of the salmon in abstraction from this essential part of its life cycle.

It is equally clear that speaking of human individuals in isolation from their social contexts makes little sense. Humans are raised in families, and the relationship between a child and its parents is fundamental to its well-being. Neither can the well-being of individuals be separated from that of their communities. Individuals who live in communities divided by disparities of wealth and opportunity often experience high levels of crime and violence. While a privileged few may prosper in such communities, the disadvantaged majority often live in desperate circumstances. But even the privileged few are less well off than they would be in a more equal and harmonious society.[11]

Individuals also cannot be isolated from the ecosystems of which they are a part. Every breath we take, every morsel of food we eat or drop of water we drink links us to the health of the air, water, and land. Humans are parts of ecosystems, interdependent with soil, plants, and other animals in complex and profound ways.

I am not completely dismissing the importance of the individual animal or human. But there is a balance to be struck between regard for the individual and regard for wider wholes. Any moral system that would accept skinning animals alive (for example) would be a very questionable ethic. But a moral system that respects only individuals and pays no attention to families, communities, species, or ecosystems is not adequate either.

The History of Individualism

The individualism of both deontological and utilitarian theories arose in a particular historical situation in which the previous non-individualistic view of human nature came under attack as oppressive.

In medieval times, humans were embedded in relationships that largely defined who they were and what they could achieve. Their obligations to their families often took precedence over their personal desires. In feudal society, the lord's obligations to his peasants and the peasants' duties to their lord restricted their personal choices. All individuals had obligations to church and monarch that further defined the available choices. This led to a fairly stable society in which all individuals had clear understandings of their roles and the expectations associated with those roles.

The attack on this view of human nature began with the Protestant Reformation. In rejecting the authority of the Roman Catholic magisterium, the reformers emphasized the free conscience of the individual and the importance of the individual's personal faith.

This emphasis on individual faith and conscience shattered religious uniformity and led to the development of religious minorities in many countries. This in turn led to devastating religious wars and persecution over the next 200 years. When it became clear that no group would be able to dominate completely, political systems that gave maximum liberty to individuals to follow their own conscience developed. The word liberty gave its name to the movement that has hereafter been known as classical liberalism.

The emphasis on individual liberty was also in reaction to having hierarchical structures in the family, community, and society defended as part of the natural order of life. Liberal political and philosophical movements were seeking liberation primarily from rigid divisions of class and aristocracy that stifled individual freedom. Conservatives believed that those structures were ordained by natural law, and that people could not rise above the class in which they were born (although it was acknowledged that people could easily fall below their class). Liberals stressed the autonomy of the individual as a way of rejecting this view of class hierarchy as "natural." Through revolutions in France and America, and social reform movements in Great Britain, these new political and philosophical movements rejected the power of royalty and nobility and made room for a middle class with greater social mobility than had been previously possible.

Later, the autonomy and dignity of the individual became the basis for important movements of racial and sexual minorities, and the independence movements in the African, Asian, and Latin American colonies.

In natural law theory, the natural function of women was widely restricted to bearing children and caring for the male members of the family, so it is not surprising that an assertion of the dignity of women as individuals apart from such social roles would be seen as liberating. The opening of opportunities for women to vote, participate in political life, pursue a variety of career opportunities, and leave abusive relationships reflected this desire for liberation. However, each of these movements toward greater individual freedoms has contributed to the development of an individualistic culture in which individualism is corroding all social relations and re-sponsibilities.

In 2000, Robert Putnam documented the decline of social capital, the ties that bind people in community. His title, *Bowling Alone,* is drawn from studies showing the decline of almost every form of community orga-nization in the United States, from bowling leagues to churches, from service clubs to sewing circles.[12] People are joining organizations less and retreating into private worlds of their own making.

One of the first to notice this trend was the French social philosopher Alexis de Tocqueville, who visited the United States in the 1830s to study democracy. He was troubled by the emergence of something different from mere selfish egoism. De Tocqueville's description of this new individualism has been quoted and summarized by a modern sociologist as follows:

"Individualism is a calm and considered feeling which disposes each citizen to isolate himself from the mass of his fellows and withdraw into the circle of family and friends; with this little society formed to his taste, he gladly leaves the greater society to look after itself... Such folk owe no man anything and hardly expect anything from anybody. They form the habit of thinking of themselves in isolation and imagine that their whole destiny is in their hands." Finally, such people come to "forget their ancestors," but also their descendants, as well as isolating themselves from their contemporaries. "Each man is forever thrown back on himself alone, and there is danger that he may be shut up in the solitude of his own heart."[13]

This individualism corrodes the very liberty that spawned it, de Tocqueville believed, because if citizens withdraw into private life, democracy is left open to despotism.

Another group of sociologists, led by Robert Bellah, identified the destructive implications of individualism for views of personhood, family life, and community. They found that the emphasis on individualism leads many modern Western people to view the meaning of their lives in terms of "breaking free from family, community, and inherited ideas." The meaning of life is "to become one's own person, almost to give birth to oneself." [14]

But what they wish to be free *from* is clearer to people than what they wish to be free *for*. Breaking free from any received tradition or community often leaves people with a sense of nihilism and without any meaning to life. Without any sense of a good (beyond freedom), moral convictions are reduced to increasingly arbitrary "values," marriage and family ties are frequently disposable, and ironically, people attempt to express their individuality by defining themselves through one or another of a variety of mass-produced brands of merchandise! Individualism is corroding almost every social bond that might link people in community and give them a sense of being a part of something larger than themselves. People are trapped in their own isolation.

It is not too surprising that a society so strongly influenced by individualism would think of animals primarily in individualistic terms. But if there is any merit to these criticisms of individualism for humans, then we should beware of imposing an inadequate view of human liberty onto other animals. As we consider how ethical theories relate to the well-being of animals and the environment, it will be important to find a more adequate balance between individual liberty and communal belonging than has been common in the modern period.

The Postmodern Challenge

Postmodernism is an intellectual and social movement that emphasizes the partial nature of any knowledge. Natural law, deontology, and utilitarianism were efforts to develop a theory of ethics that all rational people would find persuasive. All three, however, were developed by European males. Over the past century, women and non-Europeans showed that the thinking of those European males was profoundly influenced by their gender and culture and that their theories were patriarchal and parochial.

For example, the prevailing idea of rationality in the modern and pre-modern theories was of intellectual, objective, abstract reason divorced from emotional attachments or attention to the class, cultural, or social context. (The necktie strikes me as the perfect symbol of this kind of rationality, tying off the head from the heart and the rest of the body.) According to this understanding, the characteristic concerns of parents for children and family should have no influence on rational thought. It should not be surprising that women are among the strongest critics of this abstract view of rationality, because it defines their traditional roles (homemaker, mother, community volunteer) as non-rational.

A number of intellectual and social trends have come together to call into question the prevailing assumption of the modern era that reality is universally accessible through rational processes. This ongoing shift in Western culture is known as postmodernism and our age is sometimes known as the postmodern age.

One of the most important insights of postmodernism is that our world view is influenced by the society we live in. It is "socially constructed." The way of understanding the world that seems so obvious to European male Christians seems very strange to Asian Taoist women or to African animists of any gender. Business people do not see the world the same way that therapists do, and members of country clubs have different attitudes than welfare recipients. Postmodern thinking is the assertion that humans are limited in their ability to comprehend the whole truth.

While to many the insights of postmodernism seem obvious, some resist them because they feel anxious about a world without certainty. Postmodernism can be dizzying with its sense that we are standing on an unstable footing, in danger of falling into an abyss. Fundamentalisms of many kinds – religious, political, economic, or scientific – seek to find a firm foundation by claiming some privileged access to reality, whether the denial of all truth that can't meet the test of experimental evidence or the belief that a particular interpretation of some sacred writing is the only possible way to faith.

The Challenge of Relativism

While postmodern thinking is a necessary corrective to claims to know the whole truth, relativism denies any moral truth at all.

Deep and difficult differences about ethical issues exist in pluralistic societies. Because these differences are often embedded in different cultural and religious traditions to which people are deeply committed, ethical controversies can be exceedingly difficult to resolve. The absence of an ethical theory that provides a universalistic account of ethics and the spread of postmodern thought has led some people, consciously or unconsciously, to a perspective called "ethical relativism." Relativism is the view that ethical standards are nothing more than matters of custom, culture, religion, and personal feelings, and that moral appeals are meaningless. A consistent relativist would say that there is no real difference between right and wrong, and that there is no objective basis for distinguishing between Adolf Hitler and Mother Teresa.

However, very few people are willing to abandon the category of morality entirely. Many people are not consistent relativists, but resort to a relativist position temporarily out of intellectual laziness, political expediency, an unwillingness to engage issues seriously, or an ignorance of the appropriate ethical categories. Just when a moral dispute reaches the point of engaging the real issues, such people throw up their hands and exclaim, "Who's to say what is right or wrong?"

To return to our example of the Atlantic seal hunt, an ethical relativist would conclude that there is no final answer to the question of whether or not the seal hunt is wrong because there is no such thing as either right or wrong. Relativists claim that moral language is just a confusing way of expressing one's personal preferences.

If relativists were right, however, then moral claims would not arouse such passionate debate. To claim that something is wrong goes well beyond expressing a personal opinion. It makes a strong claim for others not to do it. Others must respond in one of three ways: by agreeing with the moral claim and changing their behaviour to conform to it; by disputing the moral claim; or by agreeing with it but failing to change their behaviour. This last option generates difficult and painful psychic and spiritual tension because it requires people to sacrifice their integrity by continuing to do something they believe to be wrong.

If I were to claim that it is cruel to club seals, for example, people would understand that I mean something more than that I personally prefer not to hunt seals, or that I feel sorry for seals. Matters of personal taste and preference cannot be debated, while a statement about right or wrong is something that is open to discussion because it is an appeal to criteria that are beyond personal taste. People might disagree with me about whether the hunt was cruel. We could dispute whether the seals suffer and whether the hunt violates the rights of individual seals. We might consider the hunt's effects on seal and fish populations, or whether the hunt is economically viable. We could discuss what changes (if any) in the hunt might make it more morally acceptable. Those are all issues that have been part of the public discussion about the morality of the seal hunt. But even if they disagreed with my judgment about the morality of the seal hunt, most people understand such moral claims to be more than just an expression of personal or cultural preferences. They understand that to say something is wrong is to make a profound and important claim on what we think and do. It is precisely because moral claims make such important claims on our consciences that they are disputed so vigorously and require such careful consideration.

The challenge in our postmodern context is to find ways of articulating ethical claims that avoid false claims to universality while avoiding recourse to relativism.

Chapter Three
GOOD CITIZENS OF THE EARTH: CHARACTER ETHICS

It is inconceivable to me that an ethical relation to land can exist without love, respect, and admiration for land.

Aldo Leopold[1]

Being Good

Leopold has his finger on something. His quotation on the previous page suggests that what we love, respect, and admire drives our ethical behaviour. It is part of our character. So a character-based ethical theory focuses on the fundamental source of our ethical behaviour – on what we should *be* (or at least strive to become). It attempts to articulate what makes a person good, wise, and admirable. Aristotle taught that "a good action was what a good person would do, in the way a good person would do it, for the reasons a good person would do it, in the way a good person would do it."[2] But who is such a good person? How do we identify a good person? How can we tell a good person from a bad person?

Today we usually speak of people as "good" in relation to specific social roles and responsibilities. It makes sense, for example, to speak of a person as a good husband, a good mother, or a good employee because we often have a clear idea of what it means to be good in one of those roles.

Sometimes the social understanding of "goodness" is defined narrowly in terms of conformity. Many women, for example, have experienced how the social expectation of being a "good girl" enforced conformity and stifled creative expression. A good girl, a good Christian, or a good employee is often defined in oppressive terms as a person who does not disturb the order of the family, congregation, or company by raising difficult questions or challenging the status quo. When "goodness" is understood primarily in terms of conformity, families, congregations, and companies quickly become ossified and oppressive.

Rather than emphasizing conformity, it is quite possible to define goodness to include such characteristics as wisdom, creativity, and a vision for what the family, congregation, or company could become. It is possible to define goodness in ways that allow individuals to enjoy living and working in community.

The realization that it makes sense to refer to good people in relation to specific roles and relationships opens an important possibility for ecological ethics. Ecological ethics is concerned with the roles and responsibilities of humans in relation to the ecosystems in which they are embedded. We are in relationship with many other creatures, and what it means to be a good member of an ecosystem is therefore meaningful in precisely the same way as it is meaningful to be a good husband, a good mother, or a good student.

How do we know what a good member of an ecosystem (or a good husband, mother, student, or employee, for that matter) is like? This is an important question, because without knowing what good people are like, we cannot ourselves become good, or help others become good.

Modern Virtues

Character ethics names a number of ways to recognize a good person. Aristotle and his followers attempted to describe good people by describing the virtues (good habits) and vices (bad habits) that such people possess. A modern attempt to describe the virtues that good citizens of the earth need to have has been made by Steven Bouma-Prediger, who describes virtues that can contribute to sustainability.[3]

Creation has an integrity that gives all species intrinsic value. In order to preserve non-human species and their habitats, we need the virtues of *respect* and *recep-*

tivity. Respect is "proper regard for the integrity and well-being of other creatures." Receptivity is recognition of our interdependence with other creatures and openness to their distinctiveness and integrity.

Creation is finite. In order to live within the limits of the earth's resources and systems, we need the virtues of *self-restraint* and *frugality*. Self-restraint is the ability to control our consumption. Frugality means we make efficient use of the limited goods available.

Humans are also finite, but we are tempted to think of ourselves as if we are not. We need to act cautiously, and so we need the virtues of *humility* and *honesty*. Humility lets us estimate our abilities and limits accurately. Honesty is the refusal to deceive oneself, others, or God, except where other moral commitments take precedence.

In order to sustain the capacity of living creatures to flourish and reproduce, we need the virtues of *wisdom* and *hope*. Wisdom is sound practical judgment, informed by knowledge and experience, about what will foster the fruitfulness of creation. Hope is the desire for a good future accompanied by trust that such a future will come to fruition. Hope is not the presumption that a good future will come to be without effort or suffering.

The rest and rejuvenation that land, animals, and humans need come through the virtues of *patience* and *serenity*. Patience is the ability to wait in trust, knowing that great works take time. Patience is contrasted with an impetuous fear of the future and with a timid failure to act when action is necessary. Serenity is calm dedication to worthwhile goal-directed effort.

Humans are entrusted with the responsibility of caring for the earth and its creatures, especially those most in need. To do that, we need the virtues of *benevolence* and *love*. Contrasted with malice and apathy, benevolence and love are the closely related dispositions to care for others and act on behalf of their well-being.

Life often involves conflict between competing and irreconcilable desires, interests, and rights. In order to live fairly in the midst of such conflict, we need the virtues of *justice* and *courage*. Justice is the virtue of acting fairly, of discerning when the interests and desires of humans take precedence over those of other life, or vice versa. Courage in pursuit of sustainability makes it possible to persevere in difficulty, persist in adversity, and to be resolute in the face of threat.

Such descriptions, however insightful, tend toward the abstract. One can aspire to the virtue of courage, for example, without being in the least courageous. What is critical is to *become* good.

Developing Virtue
Friendship
The best way to become good is by knowing a good person as a close friend, mentor, parent, coach, or other guide. I learn what it is to be a good parent from being in relationship with good parents. I know how to be a good pastor by being in relationship with good people who are pastors or need pastors. People are complex, however, and saints are rare. It is more likely that our friends and mentors are in quest of goodness too, rather than being fully good. The quest for goodness includes acknowledging one's failings, seeking forgiveness, and learning from failure. In sharing the quest for goodness with others in community, we help each other approach the goal.

Near where I live, there is an organization dedicated to the protection of the Peace River watershed. The organization is named Friends of the Peace. That name suggests that we can learn to be good citizens of the earth by being in close relationship with some specific natural system, by paying careful attention to it, caring for it, and defending it as we would care for and defend a close friend.

Narratives

I may be wrong in thinking my friends are good parents. I can only compare them to others in my circle of friends, so it is helpful to have wider sources of reflection against which to evaluate my judgment.

Stories and narratives (fictional or not) make up one such source. If you remember a book, movie, or story that profoundly changed the way you see the world, you may understand how a story can provide moral perspective. The epic poems of Homer encouraged warrior virtues in the ancient Greeks who heard them. Narratives are at the heart of the sacred scriptures of Jews, Christians, Muslims, Sikhs, Buddhists, and others. Jesus is remembered as a storyteller, and his parables about the kingdom of God evoked a way of seeing the world that was different from the conventional world view of his time; they continue to do so now.

Modern stories also serve as sources of moral development. The novels of Charles Dickens and Aleksandr Solzhenitsyn exposed moral horrors in Victorian England and Soviet Russia. The works of Jane Austen, Nathaniel Hawthorne, and Leo Tolstoy explore moral behaviour in very different circumstances. "The list of books that have sparked revolutions, small and large, inner and outer, is endless," writes Molly Marsh. "...With our imaginations we can put ourselves into the minds and lives of others and see from different perspectives."[4]

The novelist Doris Lessing, in accepting the 2007 Nobel Prize for literature, said, "The storyteller is deep inside every one of us. The story-maker is always with us. Let us suppose our world is ravaged by war, by the horrors that we all of us easily imagine. Let us suppose floods wash through our cities, the seas rise. But the storyteller will be there, for it is our imaginations which shape us, keep us, create us – for good and for ill. It is our stories that will re-create us when we are torn, hurt, even destroyed. It is the storyteller, the dream-maker, the myth-maker, that is our phoenix that represents us at our best, and at our most creative."[5]

Stories shape the way we see the world around us and help us to distinguish right and wrong. Truly great narratives help us recognize the complexities of good and evil in ourselves and in the world around. As we will see, narratives about healthy and degraded ecosystems can help us become good citizens of the earth.

Social Practices

We also learn to be good through social practices. Practices are complex social activities with recognizable standards of excellence; sports, farming, scientific research, and community leadership are a few examples. Whatever the practice, the pursuit of excellence in it requires the participants to develop virtues, which overflow the practice itself and become part of the person's character.

A young girl learning to figure skate, for example, must develop honesty, courage, and justice. In order to improve, she must develop openness to evaluating her own performance honestly; she must also develop the courage to take risks in learning new skills and performing in front of audiences; finally, she must learn to recognize justice in the decisions about who wins and who loses in competition. Honesty, courage, and justice are three essential dispositions required to achieve excellence, not just in figure skating, but in any complex social practice. Without developing the dispositions, it is impossible to excel at a practice.

If the developing skater confines her honesty, justice, and courage to the rink, however, she will not develop virtues in the sense of qualities of character that pervade a person's life. This sometimes happens when people see their lives as fragmented. Fortunately, the developed virtues usually overflow the practice and become pervasive, which also make it easier to excel at other practices.

Because it is important to become proficient at a practice in order to develop virtues, it is not usually possible to be a good person without being good at something. It is therefore important, for the sake of moral development, for every person to find something that they can become good at. It is, however, possible to be good at something without being a good person. A good singer might be arrogant, self-centred, cruel, and vindictive. To be truly good, a person must develop all the virtues to some degree, along with integrity, a virtue that ties all the virtues together.

Social practices such as farming, gardening, hunting, fishing, and forestry have direct impacts on the health of natural systems. When proficiency in those practices is evaluated primarily by economic criteria, economic success can often come at the expense of long-term sustainability. On the other hand, if sustainability is assumed to be the major criterion for evaluating the excellence of a farmer or fisher, then they are motivated and inspired to develop the virtues necessary to be good earth citizens. It therefore makes a big difference how social practices like farming and economics are related to each other in a community.

Tradition

Friendships, narratives, and social practices differ from culture to culture, community to community. Understandings of what makes for a good person will therefore vary from community to community, and, given the complexity of modern communities, will often vary dramatically within a community. These differences mean that every understanding of what makes for a good person is going to be dependent on a tradition.

A tradition is, in the words of Alisdair MacIntyre, "an historically extended, socially embodied argument."[6] It is socially embodied because it exists as part of a community, whether a community of figure skaters, of philosophers, of scientists, of those who speak English, or of adherents to a religious faith. A tradition is historically extended because it grows and develops through time (in contrast to traditionalism which is unbending allegiance to some imagined glorious past). According to Tom Driver, "the ability to innovate while at the same time echoing ancient custom is what keeps any tradition alive."[7] Finally, a tradition is an argument, because there are different currents within traditions, and participants in a tradition are always assessing how to negotiate those different currents. Traditions are complex, fluid, passionate arguments. Every human practice, language, scholarly discipline, or occupational group exists as part of a tradition.

So how can we know what a good person is, or how to be a good person, or what the right thing to do is? It is in community, where traditions of practices, narratives, and friendship are intermingled, that people come to understand what it means to be a good person.

Resolving Moral Differences in Community

Different traditions will often find themselves in dispute over moral questions. There is no universal principle independent of a moral tradition that can resolve these disputes. Adherents to a particular tradition will often find their reasoning unconvincing to the adherents of another tradition. So, for example, opponents of the seal hunt try to convince its practitioners of its cruelty, and the hunters try to convince the opponents of its appropriateness. Each side appeals to criteria that are not part of the other's tradition and so neither side is wholly convinced. There simply is no universal principle or ethic that will be authoritative for both communities.

Moral differences between communities can only be resolved through extended and passionate dialogue held in many different contexts, from the kitchen table to the university seminar, to the courtroom, to the ballot box. At its best, dialogue consists of listening carefully to the other's point of view while making the effort to persuade the other of our own perspective. These dialogues may sometimes last for generations before they are resolved, if they are ever resolved.

Often in such disputes, one community will find a way to assert its point of view through the acquisition of political, legal, or military power, although this often does not convince the other community of the justice of its cause. This is the case with the abortion dispute, for example, where the pro-choice community has successfully appealed to legal authorities to overturn restrictions on women's access to abortion services. But a vocal and active community opposed to abortion still exists and seeks to introduce protection for the unborn.

Sometimes, over time, one side will win over the other by the moral superiority of its arguments. The struggle of African-Americans for civil rights in the United States, for example, has been largely resolved that way, although there are still significant obstacles to full equality.

Such extended dialogue will in some situations result in the mutual transformation of both traditions, as each side comes to recognize qualities it respects in the other. This has been the case for many religious communities seeking to overcome historical animosities. Through dialogue, common action, and new institutional relationships, religious communities recognize each other as fellow participants in a wider tradition and celebrate the contributions of each to that wider tradition.

Reaching for Moral Truth

Just as the postmodern insight that none of us has more than a partial view of reality does not deny that reality exists, so the acknowledgement that ethics is tradition-dependent does not invalidate the claim that there really is a difference between right and wrong, good and bad, cruelty and generosity. Just because the proverbial troop of blind men each thought they were touching something different because they had a hand on a different part of the elephant, does not mean there is no elephant. The insight that we approach morality only from within a community does not deny that that some communities have a better grasp on moral truth than others. In fact, one important characteristic of communities with strong moral traditions is that they make a clear distinction between moral truth and their own grasp of it. This is the significance of the second commandment for ethical thought: Do not make idols (fixed representations of God). God should not be confused with our limited images of the divine; the good should not be confused with our limited comprehension of morality. But the nature of the good and the nature of God keep us striving toward them.

Barbara Brown Taylor tells of watching fireworks as part of a throng celebrating the Fourth of July. Ahead of her a little girl sat on her father's shoulders.

> Every time there was a new explosion in the sky, she reached her right hand toward it, trying to curl her fingers around the light. She did this over and over again, so that all my memories of those vastly different fireworks have the same small dark hand in them, reaching for the sky.
>
> As far as I know, she never caught a single spark, but neither did she ever stop trying.[8]

A community-dependent understanding of ethics should keep us reaching for the light of moral truth. We will never possess it, but we can never stop trying to grasp it. By engaging with new questions, engaging in dialogue with other communities, and bearing witness to our deepest convictions about what is wise, just, true, and good, we contribute to the development of the moral tradition of which we are a part. To return to the metaphor of the blind encounter with an elephant, we can't be satisfied by grasping tightly to just one part, but must let our hands explore, starting from where we began and gradually forming a picture of the whole.

Albert Schweitzer's Reverence for Life

There are two writers who have defended ethical concern for non-human life who seem to fit within the theory of character ethics, even though neither of them explicitly draws on it. The best known is Albert Schweitzer, who articulated a philosophy of "reverence for life."

Schweitzer (1875–1965) was an extraordinary man, a talented musician, historian, theologian, and physician. He is perhaps most famous for his work as a physician in West Africa, which is where he found himself during the First World War. That war shattered the widespread belief in the inevitability of progress.

Schweitzer came to believe that the way beyond such catastrophic conflicts was the development of an attitude toward life that was committed to individual and social progress. The idea of reverence for life came to him while he was travelling on a river barge on the way to see a patient. At sunset, when the barge was making its way through a herd of hippopotami, "there flashed upon my mind, unforeseen and unsought, the phrase 'reverence for life.'"

The term reverence connotes an attitude of both honour and fear. Schweitzer wrote that an ethic of "reverence for life" begins with the realization that other living things have a will-to-live similar in many ways to our own. He writes,

...the man who has become a thinking being feels a compulsion to give to every will-to-live the same reverence for life that he gives to his own. He experiences that other life in his own. He accepts as being good: to preserve life, to promote life, to raise to its highest value life which is capable of development; and as being evil: to destroy life, to injure life, to repress life which is capable of development. This is the absolute, fundamental principle of the moral... A man is ethical only when life, as such, is sacred to him, that of plants and animals as that of his fellow men, and when he devotes himself helpfully to all life that is in need of help. [9]

In recognizing the will-to-live of other living things, Schweitzer acknowledges an intrinsic, inherent value in all things, similar to Kant's recognition of the intrinsic value of other rational subjects. Living things, because of this will-to-live, are good in and of themselves. For Schweitzer, though, this does not lead to a moral imperative or set of rights and duties. His reverence for life is a basic disposition towards living things – an attitude, character trait, or habit of thought – rather than a rule.

Schweitzer acknowledges that this ethical impulse of reverence for life will lead us into tragic choices where we are "obliged to live at the cost of other life, and to incur again and again the guilt of destroying and injuring life."[10] At its most basic, to eat means to sacrifice some other life. To build a home requires the cutting of a tree. To take medicine means to take the lives of bacteria, viruses, and parasites. Such choices are tragic because the attitude of reverence does not allow us to overlook the will-to-live of those beings, or to easily dismiss the moral conflict that arises in such situations.

Schweitzer here is drawing on his Christian assumptions, for the Christian narrative makes it clear that the way things are is not the way they are intended to be. In Schweitzer's terms, "The world offers us the horrible drama of Will-to-Live divided against itself. One existence holds its own at the cost of another: one destroys another."[11]

Reverence for life keeps us open to the full implications and responsibilities of our decisions. It includes a reluctance to take, injure, or repress life without good reason, and it implies that even when we do choose to take, injure, or repress life we do so with remorse and full awareness of the tragedy of that choice.

With regard to the seal hunt, I suspect that Schweitzer would encourage the hunters to cultivate a sense of the tragic choice they are making in killing seals. Hunters should be fully aware of the will-to-live of seals and be reluctant to do them harm. If they must be killed, the killing should be done with a full sense of the tragedy of depriving a creature of its life. Schweitzer might well be willing to acknowledge that some hunting of seals is compatible with reverence for life, provided it is undertaken with full awareness of the violation of the will-to-live of other creatures, and in order to satisfy basic needs of humans, for whom we also must have reverence.

Reverence for life is a good example of a character trait or virtue, and Schweitzer's sense of the tragic choices that reverence for all life must entail is a profound insight that must not be lost in future attempts to develop an ecological ethic. Still, his proposal suffers from two major flaws. First, by asserting that all living things have a will-to-live comparable to our own, he fails to make any distinctions that might help us to resolve even admittedly tragic choices. If we are to have equal reverence for all creatures, then how could we ever take any action that would favour one over another?

Surely, however, it is possible to have reverence for life and yet acknowledge that an individual antelope deserves more respect than an individual ant, and an individual monkey deserves more respect than an individual mosquito. Such judgments can be made on the basis of our recognition of the individuality of other creatures. Plants, fungi, insects, and fish, for example, produce overwhelming numbers of spores, pollen, and eggs and provide little or no care for their offspring. It seems appropriate that our reverence for individuals of such species is less developed than for members of species that produce small numbers of offspring and invest heavily in their care. It is possible, I think, to respect the importance of ants and earthworms in ecosystems, without being too troubled about stepping on one individual. Elephants, dolphins, whales, and primates, on the other hand, live in family groups throughout their lives and even mourn their dead. Our reverence for them should therefore be of a much higher degree, and the burden of proof required to justify killing, injuring, or repressing them should be very high.

The degree of respect warranted for other individual animals, including seals and domestic livestock, can be evaluated based on where they fall in that spectrum between ants and elephants. Making these distinctions allows us to maintain a sense of reverence for individual creatures without every choice becoming equally tragic. If every action is equally tragic, no moral distinctions can be made. By having clear criteria for why killing an elephant is more tragic than swatting a mosquito, we can provide a better rationale for responding to the suffering of individual animals and protecting their rights than has been done by either Animal Liberation or Animal Rights theorists.

The second flaw in Schweitzer's ethic is that it does not describe how reverence for life might be cultivated. In the absence of narratives, practices, and a community to support this virtue, reverence for life remains a mere hint of what an ecological character ethic might entail.

Aldo Leopold and the Land Ethic

Aldo Leopold (1887–1948) was a passionate hunter who worked as a game manager for the United States Forest Service and later as a professor of game management. In his early career, he saw game animals as resources or crops that should be managed scientifically to improve the harvest. He viewed predatory animals as undesirable competition for the game animals, and supported bounty programs, poisoning, trapping, and active culls to eliminate what he called "varmints."

Two experiences changed his views dramatically. The first came in 1909, when he was hunting with some friends on a mountainside in New Mexico. They saw a mother wolf and her cubs and opened fire.

> We reached the old wolf in time to watch a fierce green fire dying in her eyes. I realized then, and have known ever since, that there was something new to me in those eyes – something known only to her and to the mountain. I was young then, and full of trigger-itch; I thought that because fewer wolves meant more deer, no wolves would mean a hunters' paradise. But after seeing the fierce green fire die, I sensed that neither the wolf nor the mountain agreed with such a view.[12]

The second experience occurred when he observed the consequences of aggressive hunting of wolves and mountain lions on the Kaibab plateau in Arizona in the 1920s. When these natural predators all but disappeared from the plateau, deer herds grew rapidly. It was not long, however, before they consumed all the foliage on the plateau and starved. "I now suspect," he wrote later, "that just as a deer herd lives in mortal fear of its wolves, so does a mountain live in mortal fear of its deer. And perhaps with better cause, for while a buck pulled down by wolves can be replaced in two or three years, a range pulled down by too many deer may fail of replacement in as many decades."[13]

As his thinking developed, and the science of ecology began to emerge, Leopold realized that he had been thinking of nature in mechanistic terms, to be managed and manipulated to meet human goals. He also came to realize that mechanistic thinking seriously underestimates the interconnectedness of ecosystems, views the land as dead (when even a handful of soil contains millions of living organisms), and presumes that nature is a tool in human hands. It also fails to recognize that we are utterly dependent on nature.

Leopold developed the image of a great "pyramid of life"[14] with soil at the base, plants next, and then additional layers of insects, birds, and rodents. Larger carnivores (including humans) are at the apex. The pyramid is held together by a complex tangle of food chains that are highly organized systems of competition and cooperation. Given the complexity of this structure, he argues that it would be foolish to discard parts that seem useless because their value in the whole may not be fully understood.

Humans have acquired such power that unless we manage the whole with a deep respect for what we know about how the pyramid is held together, and humility about what we do not know, the whole structure is threatened. Society needs to adopt a "land ethic," based on science *and* on love, respect, and reverence for the natural world. This new land ethic would encourage people to see the land as a "community to which we belong," rather than as a "commodity belonging to us."[15]

Economic self-interest assigns no value to such humility. Leopold estimated that less than five percent of the tens of thousands of plants and animals in his own state had economic value, since viewing conservation as a matter of economic self-interest ignores and eliminates many members of the land community that are essential to its healthy functioning but have no commercial value. We should be conscious that we may be completely ignorant of the importance of many vanishing species.

Conservation defined in terms of enlightened self-interest "defines no right or wrong, assigns no obligation, calls for no sacrifice, implies no change in the current philosophy of values[16]. The tendency to treat land in terms of our own economic self-interest is powerful, he says, and must be counteracted by an ethical restraint every bit as powerful as the social ethic that encourages cooperation and discourages selfish behaviour in human communities. This is a social ethic leading to "social approbation for right actions: social disapproval for wrong actions.[17] The key to such an ethic is simply to

> quit thinking about decent land-use as solely an economic problem. Examine each question in terms of what is ethically and esthetically right, as well as what is economically expedient. A thing is right when it tends to preserve the integrity, stability, and beauty of the biotic community. It is wrong when it tends otherwise.[18]

There has been much debate among philosophers about this last sentence, the most direct formulation of Leopold's ethic. Some assume that Leopold intended it as a rule, like Kant's categorical imperative, and have criticized it as inadequate. But his emphasis seems to be on a character ethic that will change the way we perceive the land and the way we think about it.[19]

It seems natural to read Leopold's land ethic as a character ethic because he gives his attention to three factors we have named as key to a character ethic: narrative, practices, and tradition. The essay in which Leopold names his land ethic is the last in a collection called *A Sand County Almanac*. The first section of the book is devoted to narratives celebrating Leopold's relationship with the biotic community on the rundown farm where he spent his weekends. As he explores this sandy patch of soil, he conveys a sense of affection and reverence for the natural abundance of even a degraded plot of land.

The second section continues the narrative mode with more sombre stories about the deterioration of the land community in many of the places he had worked. With both scientific precision and literary skill he evokes a sense of loss over the death and diminishment of the landscape. It is only in the last pages of this now-classic work that he turns to more abstract reflections. Long before he tells us that we should love, respect, and admire the pyramid of life, Leopold has led us to that love, respect, and admiration through the stories he offers. Long before he tells us that we should grieve the deterioration of the land, he has evoked it through inviting us to see it through his own eyes.

Leopold also clearly identifies the practices that cultivate desirable patterns of perception and thought. The results of the practices of scientific observation are everywhere present in his writings. He is aware of how the practices of hunting and fishing led him to perceive details of the behaviour of fish and animals, but is equally attentive to how less admirable hunting and fishing practices can degrade a sportsman's character. In his experience, as many as half of the deer hunters shot and abandoned at least one doe, fawn, or immature buck before taking a legal buck, a practice he believes "constitutes actual training for ethical depravity elsewhere." In the absence of any audience, it is only the sportsman's own conscience that dictates his action. Leopold argues that healthy ecosystems and virtuous character reinforce one another, while depraved characters and degraded ecosystems also travel in company.

Elsewhere, Leopold expresses his conviction that the practices of gardening, farming, and chopping wood have spiritual (and therefore ethical) implications. In one memorable passage, he writes,

> There are two spiritual dangers in not owning a farm. One is the danger of supposing that breakfast comes from the grocery, and the other that heat comes from the furnace.
>
> To avoid the first danger, one should plant a garden, preferably where there is no grocer to confuse the issue.
>
> To avoid the second, he should lay a split of good oak on the andirons, preferably where there is no furnace, and let it warm his shins while a February blizzard tosses the trees outside. If one has cut, split, hauled and piled his own good oak, and let his mind work the while, he will remember much about where the heat comes from, and with a wealth of detail denied to those who spend the week end in town astride a radiator.[20]

In that passage, Leopold explicitly acknowledges the impact that our everyday practices have in shaping the way we see the world. "There is value in any experience that reminds us of our dependency on the soil-plant-animal-man food chain, and of the fundamental organization of the biota. Civilization has so cluttered this elemental man-earth relation with gadgets and middlemen that awareness of it is growing dim. We fancy that industry supports us, forgetting what supports industry."[21]

Leopold is clear that he is not trying to develop a system of ethics that will persist unchanged for all time. Rather he is contributing to a tradition, or in his words, an evolutionary process that will evolve over time:

> I have purposely presented the land ethic as a product of social evolution because nothing as important as an ethic is ever "written." Only the most superficial student of history supposes that Moses "wrote" the Decalogue; it evolved in the minds of a thinking community, and Moses wrote a tentative summary of it for a "seminar." I say tentative because evolution never stops.[22]

Leopold's intuitions about the importance of narrative, practices, and tradition anticipate in prescient ways the postmodern theory of character ethics that developed decades after his death.

Good Citizens of the Earth

I have explored these ethical theories in some detail because they offer guidance as we seek a more respectful relationship with the ecosystems we inhabit. While theories focusing on natural law, consequences, rights/duties, and character are often presented as separate alternatives, each raises important issues that should be considered. It is probably better to think of them as complementary ways of thinking of ethics that wise people can draw on in different situations.

Wise people will not ignore rights, duties, or consequences as they consider challenges of environmental ethics such as those raised by the seal hunt. But in order to know what rights, duties, and consequences are to be considered and when, we need to be wise. An ecological ethic that is attentive to issues of character development will have to attend carefully to the practices of the communities in which we live, and ask how the practices that form our characters need to evolve before we can truly see ourselves as wise.

Stanley Hauerwas and John Berkman began an essay on animal rights by wondering whether it was possible to seriously consider the issue of animal rights apart from the practices of eating. One of them is a vegetarian. The other is not. That is not irrelevant to the topic, they point out, because "our practices, more than our arguments, reveal and shape what is truly important to us."[23] They wondered what the concrete practice of eating meat would mean for the topic they were discussing, and whether they could even consider the possibility that animals have rights while eating a hamburger. Sometimes talk is less important than action, in part because the practices in which we participate also shape what we can and cannot say and think. And because practices are social, and we learn them while growing up, they predate our own choices and form the ways we think, perceive, and speak.

As cultural animals, humans are trained in specific social practices. These practices shape our individual character and the character of our communities. Our habits make some things obvious to us, and prevent us from seeing other things. They point us toward thinking about the world and our lives in the world in some ways and make it harder to think about them in others. These practices are at the heart of the way we live and act as communities. It is therefore vitally important, if we are to become good citizens of ecosystems, for us to attend carefully to the social practices that shape our current ways of life, and to choose thoughtfully the practices that will help us move toward greater integrity in our relationships with the rest of creation.

Most of us engage in unsustainable practices in our work, recreation, and community life. The reason our communities are not sustainable is that many of the social practices that give them shape are unsustainable. Practices are difficult to change, however, because people have invested considerable time and effort in achieving excellence in them. People who developed a level of excellence in a social practice often experience pleasure, prestige, and economic rewards from the practice. That makes it difficult for people to abandon even clearly unsustainable practices. And it undermines any incentive to invest time and energy in new practices.

It may be hard to change, but it is not impossible. We can evaluate the sustainability of our various social practices and we can choose to develop new standards of excellence and reshape our social practices in more sustainable directions.

It is impossible to explore in one volume all of the practices affecting the sustainability of our communities. In the next chapters, however, we will explore pervasive economic, technological, and religious practices that are foundational to many other practices. These practices shape who we are: they shape the way we see ourselves and the world around us, the way we understand what is valuable and what we consider to be the reason and goal of life itself – in other words, what it means to live a "successful" life. In turn, these ways of seeing the world

determine what we consider to be worthwhile and plea-
surable, and so support sustainable or unsustainable
ways of living in the world.

Chapter Four
THE *REAL* WEALTH OF NATIONS

When shopping rather than gardening
is our primary relation to the world,
we forfeit a deep appreciation of life
as a precious gift to be gratefully received,
carefully nurtured, and generously shared.

Norman Wirzba[1]

Only after the last tree has been cut down,
Only after the last river has been poisoned,
Only after the last fish has been caught,
Only then will you find that money cannot be eaten.

anonymous Cree prophecy[2]

Pessimism Versus Optimism

In the early 19th century a prominent English economist named Thomas R. Malthus predicted that the earth's population would regularly outstrip the supply of food. Population grows exponentially because the extra people added to the population also reproduce. A population of one million will grow to two million, then four million, then eight million, and so on. Malthus predicted that food production rates would also increase, but only by a few percentages here and there. That difference in the two rates of growth led Malthus to conclude that population would only be held in check by famine, war, and disease on the one hand, or by "moral restraint" (late marriage and abstinence) on the other. Malthus' pessimistic outlook led to economics being described as the "dismal science."

Malthus' prediction of population increase was essentially correct. (In 1820 the world population reached one billion. By 1930, it had doubled to two billion. It reached four billion in 1974, six billion in 2000, and is predicted to reach between eight and ten billion by 2050.) However, it seems that Malthus failed to account for how different strategies for increasing food production reinforce each other and produce exponential growth. For much of the past few decades, food production has more than kept pace with population growth, although most recently the growth in global food production has rapidly slowed.

Since his time, Malthus' analysis has been expanded in a number of ways. First, it is now recognized that economic growth increases the per person consumption of resources, compounding the effects of population growth. Second, in addition to food production, the supply of basic resources such as wood, water, topsoil, oil, and iron ore is also limited. Third, waste production and pollution increase along with economic and population growth. Finally, the negative impacts of these factors on ecosystems and other natural systems have become significant. These observations have led to many predictions of resource scarcity and environmental destruction.

In 1972, the Club of Rome, an international team of scientists and industrialists, published a book called *The Limits to Growth*, which used computerized economic models to study trends in population, industrialization, food, consumption of nonrenewable resources (including energy), and pollution. The study found not only that all of those factors were growing individually at exponential rates, but that their interactions made that growth even more problematic. They predicted that several of these trends might converge to produce limits to growth simultaneously, making problem-solving vastly more difficult. They concluded that "if the present growth trends in world population, industrialization, pollution, food production, and resource depletion continue unchanged, the limits to growth on this planet will be reached sometime within the next one hundred years."[3] The authors compared the state of the world's economy to a vehicle driving faster and faster towards the edge of a cliff. If we don't slow down and change direction, they predict, we will go off the edge. In spite of this dire warning, however, the authors of *The Limits to Growth* were optimistic that it is possible to establish an economy that is able to satisfy the basic material requirements of the world's population and be ecologically and economically sustainable far into the future.

A variety of optimistic scholars, analysts, and commentators strongly criticize any warnings about resource limits. They argue that there are few, if any, strict limits to the growth of population or prosperity. These "economic optimists"[4] point out that limits that once appeared unavoidable have regularly proved to be manageable. They point out that nations that combine robust democratic institutions, free markets, and active research and development communities have regularly been able to solve many or all of the problems associated with limited resources.

According to these optimists, the spread of markets, science, and democracy around the world will cause living conditions to improve indefinitely. As Julian Simon wrote, "There is no physical or economic reason why human resourcefulness and enterprise cannot forever continue to respond to impending shortages and existing problems with new expedients that, after an adjustment period, leave us better off than before the problem arose."[5] The optimists account for failures by blaming inadequate markets and governance systems.

Today, the economic optimist viewpoint is widely held in business and conservative political circles. It is appealing for a number of reasons. It is true that pessimism has falsely predicted scarcity crises. It is also true that markets stimulate innovation and conservation in powerful ways, science provides new ideas, and democracy empowers involvement. Perhaps most importantly, it is appealing because to take concerns about limits seriously would require some very difficult political, economic, and ethical choices.

Will the Realists Please Stand Up?

So, who is right, the optimists or the pessimists? In coming years, the rapid economic growth of heavily populated countries like China and India will likely lead to greater demands for food, oil, wood, paper, grain, and metals.[6] In response to rising demand, prices will also rise, sometimes dramatically. In healthy markets, rising prices of a product can help to encourage conservation, additional supply, innovation, and substitution.

It is, however, not always true that rising prices help to extend a limited resource. Take wild ocean fish, for example. About two billion people depend on wild fish and seafood for protein, so there is tremendous demand. It is difficult to establish ownership rights over wild fish stocks, however, because fish have the inconvenient tendency to swim across borders. As a result, the usual incentives to conserve do not apply. Instead, as fish become scarcer and their prices rise, they become more valuable. The rising price becomes an incentive to catch more fish, more rapidly, a classic tragedy of the commons. Unless fishers and fishing nations collaborate to regulate fisheries, the consequence is almost inevitable. The failure to effectively regulate fisheries has led to a 90% decline in the world stocks of large ocean fish in the past 50 years.[7]

The example of wild fish exposes a major problem with the economic optimist perspective. Market dynamics are fairly effective at distributing and encouraging conservation of natural *resources*, but they are much less effective at conserving natural *systems* that are the foundation of the economy.

Markets work well under very specific conditions. They work well when a wide variety of producers and consumers are all interested in a product, have full information about alternatives and substitutes, and negotiate a price for that product from a position of relative equality.

But in the absence of those specific conditions, markets can fail, and for a number of reasons, including limited information, monopolies, imbalances of power between suppliers and consumers, and what economists call "externalities." Externalities occur when participants in a market do not bear all of the costs of the economic activity. No one has to pay for air, for example, so when the air is polluted, no one pays for the costs of cleanup, impacts on health, or declines in agricultural production. While producers pay the financial costs of finding and harvesting fish and oil, to take two other examples, they do not pay all the other costs involved in having the resource available.

Another market failure concerns the disproportionate impacts of rising prices on those who are least able to pay. Markets presume that everyone participates on a relatively equal footing, but the poor spend the vast amount of their limited incomes on the basics of life. For the nearly three billion people living on less than two dollars a day, increasing food prices can be devastating. For the extremely poor, rising food prices have direct effects: poorer nutrition, women at greater risk of dying in childbirth, newborns with lower birth weights, child developmental delays, greater problems with eyesight, compromised immune systems, and higher risk of child mortality. Even for those with a few more resources, rising food prices mean there is less money available for doctors, medicines, school fees and supplies. Sometimes children must work rather than go to school. In some countries, girls are withdrawn from school and sent to work rather than boys, with serious implications for those girls and their children.

Distributive Justice

Shortages of food, oil, and other resources impact the poor first. If the world is compared to a sinking boat, with the great mass of the world's poor at one end and the wealthy at the other, the poor end sinks first. But the boat still sinks.[8] The whole community is threatened, but the threat to the poor is more immediate.

So the reality of limits raises profound questions about justice. Distributive justice asks if food, health, education, clean air, clean water, and other goods and services are fairly distributed. Procedural justice asks if governments, communities, and corporations use procedures that are open, transparent, and consultative to make decisions, and if those most affected by the decisions are able to shape them.

Economic optimists avoid the distributive justice question because they believe everyone benefits from free markets and democratic governments. The world is fair, they claim, because these institutional procedures are the best.

But are they? Optimists tend to treat markets, science, and democracy as easily established cure-alls, when they are actually highly complex social institutions dependent on many variables.[9] Scientific research depends on the funding decisions of governments and corporations that usually do not give priority to the needs of the most impoverished people. And even if research is adequately funded, the mere existence of a problem does not guarantee that science will find a viable solution.[10]

Well-functioning markets require a complex set of legal, governmental, banking, and institutional supports, and even then can experience market failure. The inherent volatility of currency, credit, and stock markets can also severely undermine even healthy economies in relatively short order, as the economic crises in Asia (1997) and North America (2008) demonstrated.[11] And even a stable, well-regulated market systematically neglects the needs and hopes of the poor, because a lack of income keeps them from having an influence. Bill Gates points out, "Some needs aren't heard because, from a dollar point of view, they're not speaking loudly enough."[12] The economic system overlooks poorer people and poorer nations until they make enough fuss to become a threat. Then, instead of responding to their demands, the system resists their efforts through the use of coercive and even violent methods.[13]

Democratic governance and regulation corrects the tendency of markets to privilege private over public goods. Democracies have their own frailties, however, and even within mature democratic systems, wealthy individuals and corporations exert dramatically disproportionate influence over decision-making processes.

Democracy is only as healthy as its citizens are informed and active. There will always be pressures on governments to make decisions that privilege private interests at the cost of the public good. People must be prepared to think of themselves as citizens who can distinguish the public good from private interests, and not just as consumers. As the director of the Centre for Science and Development in India writes,

> the most important driver of environmental change in our countries is not government, laws, regulation, funds, or technology per se. It is the ability of its people to "work" its democracy. But democracy...requires careful nurturing so that the media, the judiciary, and all other organs of governance can decide in the public and not private [read corporate] interests.[14]

Even the most just procedure, however, cannot obscure the question of distributive justice raised by the vast and growing gap between the wealthy and the poor, both within and between nations. For example, hunger is largely a problem of wealth distribution. Despite the number of people who are undernourished in the world, there is lots of food. But much of it is wasted or fed to animals to produce meat.* Wealthier people are able to afford meat in quantities that vastly exceed nutritional requirements, so it becomes more lucrative for farmers to grow feed grains for animals than to grow staple foods for the poorest people.

This gap between the rich and the poor is huge and growing rapidly. Over half the population of developing countries – 2.7 *billion* people – live on less than two American dollars a day,[15] and half the world's children – a *billion* children – suffer severe deprivations of food, water, sanitation, health, shelter, and education.[16] At the other end of the scale, between 2003 and 2006 the number of the world's billionaires increased by 66 percent and their total net worth rose an astonishing 86 percent to 2.6 *trillion* dollars.[17] In other words, fewer than 800 people have approximately the same amount of money as nearly three billion people have over more than a year. I can't imagine any understanding of justice that would consider that distribution of wealth to be fair.

A holistic ethic that takes resource limits seriously comes face to face with questions of how resources are distributed and how decisions are made. When economic optimism is the dominant philosophy, ethical questions are obscured by a false faith in the ability of markets and technology to solve all the important problems. When that faith is exposed as a fiction, questions of ethics and justice become crucial.

*It takes between two and seven calories of grain to produce a single calorie of meat.

The Influence of Economics

In December 1991 the chief economist at the World Bank, Lawrence Summers, wrote an internal memo proposing that the World Bank encourage migration of dirty industries to least developed countries. Among the reasons he offered were that countries with lowest wages would have lower costs from the increased illness and deaths associated with such industries. He observed, "I think the economic logic behind dumping a load of toxic waste in the lowest wage country is impeccable and we should face up to that."[18] The memo was leaked and Summers issued the predictable apology, explaining that he intended the memo to be ironic.

The memo, however it was intended, illustrates the callousness of economic analysis when divorced from ethical, humanitarian, and environmental concerns. But this bloodless analysis drives much government planning and international development work. Indeed the idea of "development" is often defined solely in terms of economic growth, and our political life has become dominated by the belief that the good life can be quantified using economic categories.

Cultural Assumptions

Social practices, including the practice of measuring our well-being, shape the way we think, perceive, and act. So how and what we measure when considering our well-being are crucial in shaping whether we are good citizens of the earth. The increasing influence of economics in measuring well-being is based in part on the assumption that it is a value-free science that can serve as an objective measure of our progress as a society. But that is not true.

Our economic practices presume certain culturally based assumptions,[19] such as an emphasis on measurement and quantification. Something that is difficult or impossible to measure (such as moral conviction) is dismissed as a personal preference. For example, the commitment of people to wilderness preservation or clean water may be reduced to the willingness of people to pay to hike or camp in a wilderness area or to have clean water. But our willingness to pay for something is quite different from our beliefs and convictions about its importance. And because animals, impoverished people, future generations, and ecosystems are not able to pay, questions affecting their rights and well-being are systematically minimized by economic practices.

Conventional economic practices also assume that individuals care primarily about satisfying their personal wants and needs. They are not viewed as citizens who can dialogue and participate in decisions that shape our community life. Economic practices that stress individual consumer choices are therefore often at odds with the practices of democratic governance.

The hero of the modern economy, it has been pointed out, could easily be a resident of an area contaminated by toxic waste, suffering from cancer, on his way to sign his divorce papers when his car is wrecked by a tornado.[20] His divorce and health problems are generating fees for lawyers and healthcare providers. The car wreck generates income for auto body shops, insurance companies, and car manufacturers. Pollution adds to the economy twice, once through production, and then again if it is ever cleaned up. Natural disasters generate income for building contractors and home improvement stores. No one would want the life of this hero, but it is what the bloodless analysis of economic practice holds up as a good life. It is the goal to which the single-minded pursuit of economic growth leads. This has led some to call traditional economics "autistic."[21] People with autism have difficulty perceiving and understanding the complexities and subtleties of relationships and emotions. In precisely the same way, traditional economic practices suffer from an inability to recognize much of what is most important to human life. This has led to a search for alternative economic practices that point the way to a better life.

Sustainable Economics

Current models of development and economic growth place the economy at the centre and suggest that everything else – the environment, society, human well-being – rotates around that centre. We need a shift in world view so that we recognize that the economy is only a part of the whole. We need to develop an economy that respects the limits imposed by the living earth.[22]

Traditional market economics pays little attention to how natural systems produce the raw materials for our economy or absorb the waste products of it. But one study of the value of these critical "ecosystem services" estimated their worth as between 16 and 54 *trillion* American dollars, an amount far larger than the total human economy.[23]

The danger of making such an estimate is that it could support the modern assumption that everything of importance can be assessed in economic terms. How can one put a price on beauty, for example, or on the spiritual importance of a landscape to indigenous people who have inhabited it for tens of thousands of years? It would be more helpful to acknowledge that economic analysis has limits. There are some things that are acknowledged, even by the advertising of a leading credit card company, as priceless. But in an age that gives inordinate value to economic considerations, these huge numbers might serve to shock into awareness those who have no sense of any value beyond the numbers. In spite of its limitations, economics is a powerful tool for ordering our common life, and we need to find ways to reorient it so that it stands in right relationship to the environment.

Modelling Economics on Ecosystems

Our current economic system (converting raw materials into products for consumption) is linear – it moves in one direction as products are created, consumed, and then discarded when they are used up. Ecosystems, in contrast, continually recycle and reuse their wastes. The waste products from one organism serve as food for another. An economy modelled on ecosystems redesigns the linear model into a circular one. Waste products from one industry become the raw materials for another. Systems of negative feedback loops, modelled on those found in ecosystems, limit the use of natural resources and the production of wastes to the capacities of natural systems.

The difficulty with limiting economic activity to the limits of natural systems is that traditional economics sees growth as essential. Lack of growth leads to recession, or worse. In contrast, sustainable economists point out that infinite growth in a finite system is simply not possible, and by attempting to grow the economy infinitely, we are making a suicidal mistake.[24] They make a distinction between *development* and *growth*:

When something grows, it gets bigger. When something develops it gets different. The earth ecosystem develops (evolves), but it does not grow. Its subsystem, the economy, must eventually stop growing, but it can continue to develop. The term "sustainable development" therefore makes sense for the economy, but only if it is understood as "development without growth."[25]

Sustainable economists have a number of proposals designed to model economics on ecosystems. First, they propose that production in forestry, agriculture, fisheries, and other renewable resources be limited to a conservative estimate of the rate at which those resources could be replenished. Second, they suggest that production of non-renewable resources be limited to the rate at which waste products can be absorbed. Third, they suggest that some products should not be sold at all but only leased, and that the company that produces them be responsible for disposing of them responsibly. Fourth, they propose that industrial systems use the waste products and energy from one production system as inputs for another. For example, a large petrochemical plant near my home channels excess heat to local greenhouses.

The Real Costs

Perhaps the simplest way to build a sustainable economy is to have the purchase price of an item include the full environmental and social costs of the product. We rely on the market price for important signals about what to do. But if the market price does not include all the costs of a product, we are making decisions based on false information and flawed accounting. The price we pay at the pump for gasoline does not include the costs of government support of the oil industry, oil supply protection through military and regulatory means, oil spills, air pollution, travel delays due to road congestion and urban sprawl, car accidents, subsidized parking, and insurance losses due to automobile-related climate change. The International Centre for Technology Assessment estimated in 1998 that in the United States such costs amounted to between 560 *billion* and 1.7 *trillion* dollars. If the price of gasoline included those costs, it would be five to 15 times higher.[26]

If economists, government officials, and other experts worked together to include all the costs of burning gasoline or coal, of deforestation, of over-pumping aquifers, and of overfishing in taxes and surcharges, those destructive practices would be quickly and dramatically reduced. Full-cost accounting would also make the prices of wind, solar, and geothermal power more competitive.

What Is Development?

Early on the morning of November 10, 2008, a woman from the San Marcos district in Guatemala boarded a bus with her two small children and travelled for four hours to spend an hour with a group of visiting Canadians, including me. After our meeting, Christina boarded the bus for her return journey. When I learned how far Christina had come, I was astonished. Why would she devote so much time and energy to meet with our small group? As her story unfolded, it became clear that she had taken the trip to defend her community, and she was looking for allies.

Christina lives in San Miguel Ixtahuacán, a community populated mainly by Mayan indigenous people who speak the Mam language. San Miguel has been dramatically affected by the Marlin mine, a large open pit gold and silver mine operated by a subsidiary of the Canadian mining conglomerate Goldcorp Inc. While the mine has created nearly 2,000 jobs in the area since the beginning of construction in 2004,[27] it has disrupted the way of life of many more. Christina described how blasting at the mine had cracked foundations and rendered homes uninhabitable. Thirsty for water, mining operations had lowered the water table, causing the deaths of countless trees, including fruit trees that local people depend on for food. Chemicals and other by-products from the mine poisoned local water, and numerous new medical problems were reported by local people, especially children. Christina described beatings and other human rights violations of those opposing the mine.[28] While international law requires that projects developed on indigenous lands receive the free and informed prior consent of the communities affected, the mine had been developed in spite of plebiscites opposing it. Christina and her colleagues appealed to the Inter-American Commission on Human Rights, and the government of Guatemala suspended mining operations at Marlin in June 2010.

Every year, between ten and 15 million people worldwide are displaced by development projects. Many of these people do not receive adequate resettlement or compensation.[29] Around the world, mines and other "development projects" devastate local communities, yet are seen as economic boons.

Developed and Underdeveloped

The focus on economic growth as the primary measure of development dates to 1949, when the new American president, Harry Truman, spoke about the need to counter communism by addressing the "ancient enemies" of human life: hunger, misery, and despair.[30] In order to build a secure peace, Truman believed it was essential "to help the free peoples of the world, through their own efforts, to produce more food, more clothing, more materials for housing, and more mechanical power to lighten their burdens." And so Truman proposed a "bold new program for making the benefits of our scientific advances and industrial progress available for the improvement and growth of underdeveloped areas."

Truman's distinction between developed and underdeveloped areas quickly became the standard way of defining the tasks of societies and governments. Truman himself provided the defining criteria for development: "greater production is the key to prosperity and peace," and "the key to greater production is a wider and more vigorous application of modern scientific and technical knowledge." Notice, however, that in that one speech the focus shifted from relieving hunger, poverty, and misery to increasing production.

In other words, one criterion measures the degree of civilization across thousands of human cultures: its level of production. And the level of production indicates one of two categories: developed or underdeveloped. The latter came to be defined as immature versions of affluent industrialized democracies, of which the United States, in the victorious aftermath of the Second World War, was pre-eminent.

Ancient and complex cultures as diverse as India, Egypt, Ethiopia, Turkey, and Thailand were together labelled as inferior to the materially prosperous ones. The new way of defining progress swept aside culture, religion, and ethics. Material prosperity and economic production were the only matters of significance.

Measuring Development

Several decades after Truman, the focus on economic prosperity and growth has become so central to government and international planning that it is "the organizing principle for almost every society and nation on the planet."[31] Economic growth within a nation is measured by the Gross Domestic Product (GDP) indicator – a measurement of all the economic transactions that occur within a country. Governments and international aid organizations focus on increasing GDP as a sign of "development."

But GDP is a perverse way of measuring the development of a society, since it includes all economic transactions (not just the positive or productive ones), and excludes many developments that are economically invisible. The 19th-century writer John Ruskin pointed out that an economy produces "illth" as well as "wealth" but GDP lumps them both together. Increasing rates of divorce, disease, crime, alcoholism, extreme climate events, and the depletion of natural resources all end up adding to the GDP. As Walter Conable, president of World Bank, said in 1989, "Current calculations ignore the degradation of the natural-resource base and view the sale of nonrenewable resources entirely as income."[32]

Conversely, conserving resources and protecting the natural habitat are perceived to come at the expense of the economy. The unpaid work of homemakers and parents who devote time and energy to the care of children adds little or nothing to the economy. Neither do volunteer work, service clubs, block parties, community bands, gatherings of friends, parks, and a host of other activities and amenities that add immeasurably to our quality of life but do not generate economic benefits. One study shows that dancing and volunteer work rate highest when considering the things that make us happy.[33]

In traditional economies, many economic transactions take place through bartering, which GDP does not measure. Efforts to grow the GDP may undermine such alternative economies and consequently the well-being of the people. The founder of the GDP warned at the time of its creation that his measurement would give an especially inaccurate picture of traditional informal economies and should never be used for planning in such economies. This warning has been ignored by the World Bank and International Monetary Fund. Indonesia, for example, was seen as a success story during the 1970s and 1980s when its GDP grew by an average of seven percent per year. But it achieved that growth by selling its nonrenewable minerals, clear-cutting its forests, and exhausting its topsoil with intensive farming. The World Resources Institute found that the sustainable growth rate, once corrected for degraded natural capital, was only about half the official rate. And that didn't include corrections for other environmental and social costs, which would have brought the growth rate down even more.[34]

Alternative Measures of Development

As a result of these concerns, there have been repeated calls for new measurements to replace GDP as the indicator of development. In 1972, the king of Bhutan adopted a measurement called Gross National Happiness as a way of encouraging sustainable development, good governance, environmental conservation, and the promotion of cultural values.

In 1989, Herman Daly and John Cobb tracked about 20 different variables to calculate an Index of Sustainable Economic Welfare (ISEW). In 1995, the "Redefining Progress" organization developed a Genuine Progress Indicator (GPI), which tracks 51 economic, social, and environmental statistics. More recently, governmental and non-governmental agencies in Britain, Canada, Australia, and other countries have begun working on measurements of "well-being," "community vitality" and "inclusive wealth."[35] These indicators begin with a measurement of household and personal consumption and add the value of infrastructure, unpaid work, and public goods as positive contributions to economic welfare. They then subtract for lost leisure time, family breakdown, commuting time, underemployment, crime, auto accidents, pollution, and the depletion of natural resources, and adjust for income inequality, net capital formation, and net foreign borrowing. These data are available in modern industrialized economies and can easily be accumulated and converted into a measurement of real progress. So far, however, indicators like the ones described here have yet to be widely reported in the media, or have the impact on policymakers that they should.

In the United States, Canada, Europe, and Japan, measurements of genuine progress show that social well-being peaked around 1973 and declined after, even while their economies surged. In the United States, the proportion of people who reported they were very happy peaked in the 1950s. As David Holmes notes, those of us who have grown more prosperous "seem unable to enjoy our prosperity; instead we seem trapped in busyness, dissatisfied with life, isolated, and afraid."[36] In country after country, economic growth has been accompanied by dramatic increases in alcoholism, suicide, crime, anxiety, and depression.[37] "The Genuine Progress Indicator gives concrete expression to something many Canadians and Americans sense about the economy: that we live off natural, human, and social capital. We cannibalize both the social structure and the natural habitat to keep the GDP growing at the rate experts and money markets deem necessary."[38]

Just as the Copernican revolution shifted the world view of the relationship between the sun and the earth, these proposals to change our practices of measurement hint at a similar kind of shift in our world view. New methods of measurement propose that we put the good life – the well-being of people, healthy communities, and thriving ecosystems – at the centre of our understanding of growth and progress. If we get the practices of measurement right, we will find it easier to pursue the good life.

But what do we measure and how do the measurements correlate with each other? For example, should we include cultural and spiritual values, as in the Bhutanese measurement of Gross National Happiness? If so, how do we measure such values? How do we relate measurements of different categories to each other? Isn't comparing environmental degradation to income inequality a bit like comparing apples and oranges?

I raise these questions not to discourage the effort, but to point out that measuring progress and development are not value-free questions that can be answered by technical analysis, but value-laden questions that inevitably involve us in addressing ethical questions in ethical terms. Questions about how much value we place on social, environmental, and economic indicators are ethically loaded. They require us to think carefully about what we want for ourselves, our families, and our communities.

The answers depend on the traditions of particular communities. What the people of a North American city regard as an improvement in their quality of life might be quite different from what the inhabitants of a rural

African village or a South American shanty town call betterment.

No community is homogeneous either. Differences within communities lead to vigorous disputes about what actually improves lives. Communities have to work through and resolve difficult political, ideological, philosophical, and religious questions when considering their own development. Empowering participatory processes by which local communities can work toward compromise and consensus on what development will mean in their communities is crucial. Communities experience development that is defined and controlled from the outside as imperialist and colonialist.

I noted in a previous chapter that the health of forests, watersheds, marine ecosystems, and the like depends on the ability of communities to craft management systems that are intimately responsive to natural systems. Yet development defined primarily through economic analysis will often undermine the ability of communities to relate in sustainable ways to fragile natural systems.

The ability of local communities to choose their own futures is undermined through a globalization agenda being aggressively pursued through trade agreements and international institutions heavily influenced by neoliberal economic agendas. Such agreements are helpful when they reduce corruption and improve legal and financial institutions. Often, however, these agreements and institutions severely limit the ability of local communities to define development in terms of their own ethical traditions and their often intimate relationships with local ecosystems. The agreements are usually beneficial to the economic elite but often make the plight of the most impoverished people dramatically worse.

Chapter Five
SCIENCE, HUBRIS, AND HUMILITY

To reduce life to the scope of our understanding... is inevitably to enslave it, make property of it, and put it up for sale.

Wendell Berry[1]

...to allow mystery, which is to say to yourself, "There could be more, there could be things we don't understand," is not to damn knowledge.

Barry Lopez[2]

The Scientific Revolution

Science is one of the most important social practices in our society. Before the scientific revolution, people invested the world with spiritual significance and believed nature had a purpose. But in the 16th century, science became the investigation of cause and effect relationships. It was assumed that an object or creature could be fully understood through explaining what caused it. Understanding the cause allows the scientist to intervene and control the object. Nature came to be seen as a machine, a mechanism like a clock, which could be disassembled into its component parts and then manipulated to do the engineer's bidding.[3]

Francis Bacon (1561–1626), considered the founder of scientific method, was quite clear that science was about the mastery of nature for human benefit. The view that science was the pursuit of power over nature was also articulated by René Descartes (1596–1650), who wrote, "knowing the nature and behaviour of fire, water, air, stars, the heavens, and all the other bodies which surround us, as well as we now understand the different skills of our workers, we can employ these entities for all the purposes for which they are suited, and so make ourselves masters and possessors of nature."[4]

This understanding of the purpose of the scientific quest persists. To provide only one example, the 1982 report of an American commission on the ethics of medical technology concluded that "human beings have not merely the right but the duty to employ their God-given powers to harness nature for human benefit."[5]

Much scientific research still assumes that humans are the masters of an often unruly servant. Military metaphors are used to speak of "wars" and "battles" against cancer, weeds, and mosquitoes. We refer to nature as something to be harnessed, controlled, and manipulated for human benefit.

The question that needs to be asked about the power of scientific method is whether the human relationship to the rest of creation is fundamentally distorted by a method that sees that relationship primarily as one of control and mastery. As Martin Heidegger observed, when the truth that is sought in science is the power to control, the other is not allowed to stand in its own truth. Rather, it is a very specific kind of truth that is sought.[6] There may be forms of truth not amenable to current understandings of the scientific quest.

I recognized one example of this while watching humpback whales during breeding season recently on the west coast of Mexico. A three-week-old baby was cavorting, rolling on its side, flapping its flukes, flicking its tail energetically while diving, and breeching. The wildlife interpreter explained that the reason the young whale was doing this was to build its swimming muscles.

I thought at the time that such an explanation for the behaviour of the juvenile whale did not do it justice. To me, it looked very much like that young whale was having fun. But the technocratic view of nature has great difficulty dealing with the subjective experience of creatures, and so tends to ignore it.[7] Is it possible that whales experience play quite differently from the way that a biologist might describe it? Is it possible that there is a depth of mystery to a whale that cannot be explained, but only pondered?

Such one-dimensionality is quite common in popular scientific writing and programming, especially when describing the characteristics and behaviour of animals. The play of the humpback whale calf can be explained in terms of its contribution to evolutionary success: the calf finds it fun because whales have evolved so that they enjoy what contributes to their ability to compete for food and success in breeding. I do not dispute that explanation. I only question whether it is the *only* way of understanding the play of whale calves.

As Barry Lopez says, "to allow mystery...is not to damn knowledge."[8] To admit the possibility that scientific explanations do not exhaust the mystery of other beings is not to reject the value of scientific knowledge. Cultivating that sense of mystery can, in Heidegger's terms, create a "clearing" in which we have some freedom from the master-servant perspective. In that clearing, we place scientific knowledge in perspective.

I am proposing a style of thinking that is always off-balance, a movement of thought that seeks understanding even as it constantly reminds itself of how much it does not understand, "eager to learn, but knowing nothing," in John Calvin's words.[9] This dialectical style of thought, closely related to the virtue of humility, serves as the basis for a style of relationship that is both exploratory and tentative, seeking to learn, but constantly reminding itself that its understandings are at best partial and at worst deeply distorting.[10]

Reductionism

By isolating one aspect of a complex organism or system, science seeks to understand it as fully as possible. The assumption is that the whole can be understood by understanding its parts. This method is generally termed reductionism, and it has a number of dangers.

In undertaking research, scientists propose a simplified model of reality to explain certain phenomena. They then test that model through carefully designed experiments. If the experiments support the model, then it is held to be an adequate abstraction of reality. But the results of this abstraction are often confused with reality itself. Joseph Weizenbaum, an information scientist at MIT, suggests that "the very success of science has induced us first to confuse the abstract with the real, and then to forget how to make the distinction at all."[11] Thus, a scientific view of reality becomes the main view of reality and in some cases the only worthwhile view of reality. Other possible views of reality, such as poetic, artistic, moral, or spiritual approaches, are ruled inferior or antiquated. The result is that science often has difficulty finding common ground on which to communicate and work with other disciplines. This also contributes to the persistent attitude that women cannot be good scientists because they are assumed to be unable to cut themselves off from other aspects of life.[12]

Although scientists themselves may be sensitive to the limitations of their models and abstractions, they may be expected to simplify their findings to make them useful for technological and economic development. If animals and systems behave in predictable, manageable ways they are much easier to manage and control. But as the failures of marine fisheries have taught us, complex systems often do not follow such rules.

The most serious problem with reductionist science is that as more comes to be known about individual phenomena, individual scientists must specialize. They know more and more about less and less. As a result, science has fragmented into disciplines and sub-disciplines and sub-sub-disciplines. A farming magazine once tried to find a scientist who would describe for its readers the interactions in a single square yard of prairie soil. They were unable to find someone who felt competent to do so: the geologists could describe the mineral content, entomologists could write about the insect life, microbiologists understood the bacterial life, and botanists could do a passable job of the plant life, but no one could do it all.

The implications of this on our understanding of ecological concerns are profound. Even with extensive knowledge of one aspect of a complex system, no one can predict what effects manipulating a part will have on the whole. And chaos science tells us that tiny differences can have far-reaching consequences. So, increasingly, efforts to solve one problem lead to several others. These limitations suggest that it would be wise to be more cautious than we have often been when developing new technologies that have environmental impacts.

Subjects and Objects

Scientific method as it developed in the 16th century treated non-human creatures as pure objects, without any function or purpose apart from what humans made of them. Humans, however, were still considered to be unique subjects, with the power to choose. Objects had no choice about what happened to them. Objects, when acted upon, reacted in predictable ways, but subjects were not readily manipulated (and to manipulate them was to demean their status as subjects).

The separation of subject and object, and the sense of the predictability of non-human creation began to break down with the development of nuclear physics in the early 20th century. Heisenberg discovered that the method of observation of electron movement influenced the result and formulated his "uncertainty theorem." That theorem was controversial because it challenged one of the fundamental assumptions of science – that aspects of reality could be predicted. If atomic structure could not be predicted, neither could it be controlled with any precision.

As the assumptions about the predictability of non-human creation broke down, it began to become clear that non-human animals are not mere objects. Field biology began to demonstrate that individual animals have personalities and character traits that cannot be reduced to pure reaction to stimuli. Some mammals have rudimentary forms of language, and others, especially primates, dolphins, whales, and elephants, are conscious of themselves as individuals. Many animals are capable of making choices. In short, they have elements of subjectivity.

Finally, and perhaps most significantly, the distinction between humans and other animals broke down. Evolutionary biology revealed that humans are not as distinct from other animals as had long been assumed. Ecological science also revealed species interrelatedness and interdependence. As a result, humans began to be aware that we are not so much above and apart from nature as inextricably bound up with it. But if humans are part of nature, are we subjects or objects?

Power and Control

If technology is about the mastery and control of nature then it is not surprising that humans, as part of nature, also become the objects of scientific research. When humans become the objects of genetic manipulation in medicine and social research in politics and marketing, important ethical questions naturally arise: what values and objectives are being served? Whose values and objectives are being served? Are individuals or communities being technologically manipulated for their own sakes and in accordance with their deepest values, or for the sake of those who hold the economic and political power to pay for the technology? Who gets to decide what kinds of research will be done or not done and what technologies will be used or not used?

Scientific knowledge is not just power of humans over nature, but power in the hands of some humans over others. The use of science for military purposes is the most extreme example. The vast majority of scientists now work either on military projects or for commercial enterprises. Their science is intended to help make their employers more powerful and competitive.

Another example of power in the hands of some humans over others is the process by which large areas of life are quantified and defined so that they are available to anyone with the proper training. Fast food restaurants and automobile factories break down complex responsibilities into precisely defined functions, for which people can be easily trained. And because they can be easily trained, they can be easily replaced. The process of learning the technology involves suppressing one's individual characteristics, emotions, creativity, and initiative in order to accommodate oneself to the technology.[13]

Huston Smith refers to a society based on role behaviour as follows.

Society has become an impersonal mechanism and with its increasing complexity is growing more impersonal daily. More and more our lives are consumed by role behaviour, that is, behaviour in which *what* is done, not *who* is doing it, is the important factor. Since within roles persons are interchangeable – any number of persons could fill the role of bus driver or bank teller without affecting the character of the roles themselves – the more our lives are defined in terms of roles, the more our individuality idles, or rather never comes into being at all.[14]

Smith's point is especially important in a world where farmers and fishers who depend on the health of ecological resources are dominated by technological systems run by bankers and corporate managers concerned with technical efficiency and monetary profit. Farming and fishing are increasingly seen as roles rather than as vocations requiring a deep knowledge of the land or the sea.

Several writers have described our current world as controlled by a system in which technology has an extraordinarily powerful place. Jacques Ellul[15] argues that our society is so dominated by the push for efficiency that virtually all other human values are crowded out, displaced because they cannot be quantified. Neil Postman[16] points out how technology has become a kind of system of faith that assumes all problems are technical ones, and one that demands technical efficiency takes precedence over all other concerns. As John Kenneth Galbraith notes, "technology, has, so to speak, a life of its own that causes it, like some fairly elaborate monstrous organism, to batten on whatever is in its way and to assume forms that are not only inhuman but subjugate all human purposes to its own requirements."[17]

The irony of this is that a supposedly value-free technology has become our primary value. Even the word "value" implies an economic measurement, and it is increasingly supplanting more substantive moral terms like convictions, ideals, principles, and standards. So instead of technical expertise serving human goals, technical efficiency defines the human enterprise in ways that obscure other important human convictions and goals.

A New Paradigm

A paradigm is a relatively stable way of seeing the world; a model of reality that persists even when there is evidence against it. A revolution occurs when the evidence for a new paradigm or model is so persuasive that it can no longer be ignored. Even then, adherents to the old paradigm may just have to die off before the new one is accepted universally. The paradigm of science as mastery and control over nature may persist long after we have ample evidence that we need a different way of thinking about nature and human nature.

The historical roots of the scientific method in a culture that emphasizes mastery of a mechanical nature, the extent to which science is embedded in systems of power, and the reductionism by which it is pursued should make us appropriately critical of science and technology. By appropriately critical, I do not mean that we throw the baby out with the bathwater and reject science completely (if that were even possible), or that we should be unduly skeptical about findings supported by abundant evidence and a strong consensus of the scientific community.[18] I mean that we respect scientific results and conclusions as more or less complete pictures of reality, the best that we can do for now. I also mean that we should be appropriately critical of the power dynamics that drive science, and aware of the social and economic interests that any scientific claim serves.

An appropriately critical attitude to science suggests that questions of public policy or ethics cannot be addressed by scientific analysis alone. Science needs to be supplemented by philosophical, theological, ethical, and cultural considerations, including a consideration of the economic and political interests served by any given policy decision. Above all, when it comes to the natural world (including ourselves), we must preserve both a healthy respect for the mysterious depths of complexity not yet plumbed by scientific investigation, and a large dose of humility about the ability of even the most brilliant to predict the consequences of our actions.

The writer Barry Lopez artfully exemplifies this multifaceted approach to understanding. In his writings about wolves and the Arctic, Lopez carefully catalogues all the scientific information he can find on a subject, but continually reminds himself and the reader of how much more is not known. So, for example, even while presenting the results of biological studies on wolves, he points out that the total amount of time that biologists have spent observing any single wolf is only about 0.003% of the actual life experience of a wolf. Human experience of wolves is little more than a distant howl, droppings laced with animal fur, a flash of fur in the brush, and yet we in our hubris pretend to understand them![19]

Agricultural scientist Wes Jackson makes a forthright declaration of ignorance: "Since we're billions of times more ignorant than knowledgeable, why not go with our long suit and have an ignorance-based world view?"[20] Jackson believes that the ecological crisis is the result of "a knowledge-based worldview founded on the assumption that we can accumulate enough knowledge to bend nature pliantly and to run the world," and proposes "regarding informed ignorance as an apt description of the human condition and the appropriate result of a good education."[21]

Biblical scholar Ellen Davis points out that the wisdom tradition in the Bible teaches "what underlies moral failure is not simple ignorance but... a culpable pride, a destructive lack of humility."[22] The biblical wisdom teachers valued knowledge and encouraged seeking it from many sources. But they kept this within a dialectic, observing limits to human knowledge. Such willingness to accept the human condition of ignorance is what the biblical sages call "the fear of the Lord," which is "the beginning of wisdom" (Proverbs 1:7). The fear of the Lord is to preserve a sense of a mystery at the heart of things. It is to reject arrogance, pride, and intellectual dishonesty, while still appreciating that divine wisdom is rooted in creation and can be sought and appreciated.

What might science look like if it were humbled by this dialectic between curiosity and humility? In her book *Biomimicry: Innovation Inspired by Nature,* biologist Janine M. Benyus introduces an alternative approach to science in which technology approaches nature as "model, measure, and mentor." Benyus describes many examples of research that seek to model themselves after and learn from the natural world: modelling agricultural practices after prairie ecosystems and tropical forests, creating solar cells based on designs inspired by the leaves of green plants, using natural marshes to clean urban sewage, and restoring prairies and forests by mimicking wildfire and natural cutting.

But just as important are the social practices that Benyus sees as contributing to the process of learning from nature:

- *Quieting* – immersing ourselves in nature in non-manipulative ways so that we can be receptive to the wisdom of the natural world;

- *Listening* – learning as much as we can about the flora and fauna of our planet so that, in an imaginative process, nature's designs and processes can be matched to the needs of technologists and engineers;
- *Echoing* – interdisciplinary collaboration between biologists and engineers about applications of natural systems;
- *Stewarding* – preserving life's diversity and genius.[23]

These practices are both individual and social. School systems need to immerse children in nature just as much as individual adults need to choose to immerse themselves. Biological wisdom needs to be shared with engineers and technologists through the efforts of individual scientists and the development of interdisciplinary institutions in government, corporations, and universities. The development of such social practices and institutions would do much to overcome the legacy of a medieval science predicated on the assumption that the human calling is to dominate nature rather than participate in it respectfully.

Chapter Six
STEWARDING THE SACRED

There are no unsacred places;
there are only sacred places
and desecrated places.

Wendell Berry[1]

O Lord, the earth is full of your creatures.
They all look to you to give them their food in
  due season;
when you give to them, they gather it up;
when you open your hand, they are filled with
  good things.

Psalm 104

An Open Letter

In January 1990, thirty-two internationally respected scientists, led by Carl Sagan and Hans Bethe, issued "An Open Letter to the Religious Community."[2] After describing global climate change, deforestation, the extinction of species, and the possibility of global nuclear war as "what in religious language [are] sometimes called 'crimes against creation,'" the scientists expressed their conviction that

> problems of such magnitude and solutions demanding so broad a perspective must be recognized from the outset as having a religious as well as a scientific dimension. Mindful of our common responsibility, we scientists – many of us long engaged in combatting the environmental crisis – urgently appeal to the world religious community to commit, in word and deed, and as boldly as required, to preserve the environment of the Earth.

The open letter asserts that while some problems can be addressed relatively easily by technical and political means, other essential changes such as "conversion from fossil fuels to a nonpolluting energy economy, a continuing swift reversal of the nuclear arms race, and a voluntary halt to world population growth," will meet "widespread inertia, denial, and resistance."

The scientists expressed their conviction that both religion and science have vital roles to play in changing problematic behaviour because they recognized that religious communities make important contributions to questions of peace, human rights, and social justice, and influence both public policy and individual behaviour. We can use science to identify problems and viable solutions, but without a much wider sense that our planetary home is valuable, even sacred, we will not follow through with efforts to preserve it.

> As scientists, many of us have had profound experiences of awe and reverence before the universe. We understand that what is regarded as sacred is more likely to be treated with care and respect. Our planetary home should be so regarded. Efforts to safeguard and cherish the environment need to be infused with a vision of the sacred.

Sagan and his colleagues acknowledge that religious systems bring together the personal, societal, and physical realms and can thus transform individuals and society at the same time. If, as David Holmes points out, "we focus on institutional change but remain the same ourselves, we will tend to rebuild society in our own unredeemed image. Similarly, if we focus on individual renewal without at the same time reshaping our institutions, the structure and ethos of society will constantly undermine any individual change."[3]

Perhaps these scientists are simply being pragmatic in recognizing the power of religious institutions (especially in the United States) and feeling a need to engage an important cultural force on behalf of their urgent agenda. But I think their insight that religion and science each have roles to play is more profound than simple pragmatism.

They see that we need wisdom from many sources when facing the challenges before us. Reality is many faceted; looking at the world from just one angle cannot exhaust its complexity. A group of scientists and theologians brought together by the World Council of Churches said that churchmen cannot expect precedents from the past to provide answers to questions never asked in the past. On the other hand, new scientific advances do not determine what are worthy human goals. Ethical decisions in uncharted areas require that scientific capabilities be understood and used by persons and communities sensitive to their own deepest convictions about human nature and destiny. There is no sound ethical judgment on these matters independent of scientific knowledge, but science does not itself prescribe the good.[4]

Masanobu Fukuoka, a pioneer of sustainable agriculture in Japan, makes a similar point:

The point must be reached when scientists, politicians, artists, philosophers, men of religion, and all those who work in the fields should gather here, gaze out over these fields, and talk things over together. I think this is the kind of thing that must happen if people are to see beyond their specialities.... An object seen in isolation from the whole is not the real thing.[5]

A Constellation of Knowledge

The philosopher Theodore Adorno proposed the constellation as a metaphor for the many forms of knowledge we need.[6] Any being or object exists in a network of relationships. A tree, for example, is related to the sun, the atmosphere, the soil, the birds, insects, animals, and other plants that live in it and around it, and to the humans who view it as part of a sacred grove or as an economic resource. But these relationships are not peripheral to its identity. The tree cannot be understood apart from all the factors that determine its possibilities: the soil that provides its nutrients, the birds and squirrels that distribute its seeds, the sun and the air that give it life, the influences of seasons, wind, altitude, or human cultivation. The tree exists in a constellation of relationships and cannot be understood apart from them. In Adorno's words, a thing is a "crystallization" of its relationships with other things.[7] There is, therefore, an inherent complexity and multiplicity at the core of any being. There is a depth to a tree that cannot be grasped using only one form of knowledge. Each form of knowledge reveals some things and obscures others, so the fullest depth of a being cannot be revealed with only one means of knowing.

Adorno was, in addition to his philosophical work, a musicologist, so he was very interested in the ways in which the arts help us to cultivate ways of knowing that cannot be expressed in other ways. Some things can be expressed in music, others in dance, others in poetry, and others in the languages of spirituality and religion. We need to cultivate a pluralism of mind[8] – one that is open to many different forms of knowing – that understands that no matter how much we know, there remains a depth that we cannot fully plumb.

The Sacred Earth

It is this depth to which I think Carl Sagan and his associates gesture in their open letter when they speak of experiences of wonder, awe, and reverence. They are groping toward a way of acknowledging something that cannot be expressed in scientific or humanistic terms.

The scientists used the word sacred, which can mean something is

- highly valued and important
- entitled to respect
- entitled to reverence
- related to the divine
- divine itself.

Most Christian leaders would support the sacredness of the earth in the first four of these meanings, but would object to the last, as Christian theology distinguishes between the creature and the Creator. God is related to all of creation, but that does not mean that the earth is itself divine. In theological terms, this is the difference between pan-theism (the belief that all things *are* divine) and pan-en-theism (the conviction that the divine is *in* all things). That distinction has important ethical implications. To worship something is to assign it ultimate value. If creatures are worshipped as divine (pantheism) then they are assigned ultimate value in a way that may elevate them above other creatures. The Christian insistence that the divine is distinct from the creation and that worship should be reserved for the Creator (panentheism) permits respect for all things in proportion without assigning any ultimate value.

Some might object to the suggestion that the earth is entitled to reverence if reverence is understood to imply worship.[9] However, reverence can easily be understood as recognition of a mysterious depth inherent in all things, a realization that even the simplest object or reality cannot be understood in its totality.

The importance that the scientists place on the religious insight that the earth is sacred echoes a widely shared view that ecological problems arise not just from

economic and technological practices, but also from religious ones. "The more deeply I search for the roots of
the global environmental crisis," wrote former American vice-president Al Gore, "the more I am convinced
that it is an outer manifestation of an inner crisis that
is, for lack of a better word, spiritual."[10] By the word
"spiritual," Gore says that he means "the collection of
values and assumptions that determine our basic understanding of how we fit into the universe." "We have misunderstood who we are," he continues, "how we relate
to our place within creation, and why our very existence
assigns us a duty of moral alertness to the consequences
of what we do."[11]

Christian Views of Our Place in Creation

Perhaps the most influential exploration of the impact of
spirituality on environmental problems was written by
historian Lynn White, Jr.,[12] who explores how Christian
theology participated in developing the Western world
view so implicated in ecological destruction. White does
not say that Christian theology is directly and solely responsible for the ecological crisis, but makes a more nu-
anced argument that theological beliefs helped to shape
an intellectual environment in which this crisis was
possible. White traces the technological and scientific
dominance of the West to a cluster of beliefs inherent
in Western Christianity, of which the most important
was that all of nature was planned "explicitly for man's
benefit and rule: no item in the physical creation had any
purpose save to serve man's purposes." The view that
only humans have ethical significance is called anthropocentrism. White concludes, "Christianity is the most
anthropocentric religion the world has seen."

White is correct in saying that certain trends in Western Christianity contributed to the ecological crisis, but he is wrong in saying that anthropocentrism is inherent to the faith. In the biblical story of creation the phrase "and God saw that it was good" appears at many stages, and long before humans appear on the scene. The story conveys a sense of God's delight and approval of the goodness of non-human creation and its independent relationship with the creator. Influenced by that story, there existed through much of the Christian theological tradition a widely held reverence for the presence of the sacred in all of creation. The beautiful prayer of Basil the Great which serves as the epigraph for chapter two, stands as a clear example of that. The last sentence of that prayer – "May we realize that [animals] live not for us alone but for themselves and for thee, and that they love the sweetness of life" – explicitly rejects an anthropocentric view.

The intensive anthropocentric focus of the Western world emerged during the scientific revolution, when the dominant moral thought of the Western world separated from its theological roots and turned into a kind of reverent humanism, and an economic system that glorified the accumulation of wealth replaced the traditional suspicion of material prosperity. When the idea that the rest of creation exists for human benefit is embodied in our technological and economic practices, the idea gains tremendous momentum. The idea and the practices feed off each other.

Wendell Berry summarizes this point nicely when he asks,

> Could we have destroyed so much of the material creation without first learning to see it as an economic "resource" devoid of religious signifi-

cance? Could we have developed a reductionist science subserving economic violence without first developing a reductionist religion?[13]

The ethical and philosophical assumptions that guide society in important ways are rooted in religious and theological beliefs and practices. In a secular culture we may not realize the importance of these assumptions until it becomes clear they are problematic. Then, we must ask how each religion responds to the concerns raised by ecological problems, or more properly, how specific religious communities develop a local orientation and local practice that helps them live respectfully and sustainably in their local ecosystems.[14]

Religious traditions have deep reserves of symbol, myth, narrative, and ethical teaching. They often have the depth to address new questions and challenges in surprising and healing ways. In his study of societies undergoing rapid change, the sociologist Howard Becker found that the most creative leadership was offered not by those who abandoned all ties to older tradition, or by those who simply reasserted the value of those traditions, but by those he termed "sacred strangers in secular society."[15] These sacred strangers were those who approached both the new situation and the tradition with freedom and creativity. They revered and valued traditions and often reinterpreted and recast them in ways that provided new vision to meet the demands of the present. Such sacred strangers participated fully in in the freedom and openness of secular societies but were not captured by secular values. Such sacred strangers illustrate that individual religions are diverse and varied.

Just as diverse ecosystems tend to have great reserves of resiliency, diverse traditions can also often find resources to respond to new challenges. This is as true of Christianity as of any other faith tradition. In exploring the theological issues raised by these challenges, we will find that there are many resources to nurture faith, hope, and ecological sensitivity.

Because religions are communities of narrative and practice, learning a religion is more than just learning a few facts. There is a Sufi saying that there are three ways to learn about fire: we can hear about it, or we can see it, but to really learn about fire, we have to be burned by it. In the same way, to really learn about a religious tradition, we have to enter into the practices and be touched and transformed by them.

My intention here and in the next chapters is to focus on practices that have deep roots in the biblical and theological traditions and on how they contribute toward a vision of Earth's sacredness and the efforts to preserve our home. Ideas are important, but until they are embodied in social practices and institutions, they remain in the realm of theory.

I explore how the practice of stewardship invites us to image God by developing practices of kindly use for particular land and communities. In the next chapter we look at prayer. Ritual prayer, as the central act of a religious community, expresses a vision of the sacred in words and deeds. At their best, these visions of the sacred can sustain communities in their resistance to economic and technocratic power. Prayers of lament express grief, sadness, and anger over the despoliation of communities and natural systems, and prayers of confession allow us to accept responsibility for the degradation of natural systems, the extinction of species, and the suffering of individual creatures. In the final chapter, as part of an exploration of how we practice hope, we examine the practices of forming anticipatory communities, observing a day of rest, and laughter.

The Practice of Stewardship

As a Boy Scout I learned a simple ethic from my scout leaders: Always leave the campsite cleaner than it was when I found it. I was taught that the campsite was not mine to do with as I wished, but a place I inhabited briefly on the condition I cared for it. I do not remember being taught the term "stewardship," but what I learned while camping with my scout troop still serves as a valuable ethic for life: We inhabit this world only briefly, and it is not ours to do with as we wish.

Although the concept of stewardship is rooted in a theological world view, it is familiar in our secular society because we are legally and morally accountable for our actions. But our culture has a shallower understanding of stewardship than other cultures, and to recover a deep practice of stewardship it is necessary to understand why.

The word steward means essentially the same thing as the word manager. A steward is someone who manages property on behalf of the owner and is responsible to that owner. A steward receives property in trust, and the assumption of trust implies that the property will be used only for those purposes the owner intends.

There is a long Christian theological tradition that says that everything belongs to God – "the earth is the Lord's and the fullness thereof." Everything we have is given to us in trust and God holds us accountable for what we do with it, just as any owner expects an accounting from a manager.

Our understanding of stewardship, therefore, is influenced by our understanding of God, and by our cultural understanding of property. If we see God as removed and separate from the rest of creation, then we will tend to think of the rest of creation as nothing more than natural resources and commodities, removed and separate from us and God. When we think that the rest of creation has spiritual significance and its own relationship with the Creator, then our sense of stewardship changes too. Our culture sees land and property as commodities and so has a very different understanding of stewardship than a culture where people and land are bound together with God in an intimate relationship.

The Agrarian Movement

The agrarian movement arose in recent decades as a reaction to the dominant practice of industrial agriculture, which treats land as a commodity. Such industrial agriculture thrives, at least in the short term, on relatively flat areas where the climate changes only slightly over large distances. Even in such areas, however, local knowledge is important, as I learned from my prairie neighbours who have watched the wind and rainfall gauges carefully over decades and know that the land ten miles east of town is significantly drier than that ten miles north of town.[16] The wiser of them also know that the soil can be blown away in a high wind, and that to prevent erosion, trees serve an important role as windbreaks and are best carefully tended. I have learned from them the truth of what Ellen Davis says, that "agriculture has an ineluctably ethical dimension."

Our largest and most indispensible industry, food production entails at every stage judgments and practices that bear directly on the health of the earth and living creatures, on the emotional, economic and physical well-being of families and communities, and ultimately on their survival. Therefore, sound agricultural practice depends upon knowledge that is at one and the same time chemical and biological, economic, cultural, philosophical, and (following the understanding of most farmers in most places and times) religious. Agriculture involves questions of value and therefore of moral choice, whether or not we care to admit it.[17]

One farm family I know carefully tended the soil on their land against erosion for six decades. As part of their stewardship of the soil, this family nurtured stands of trees as windbreaks. When the time came for the second generation on this farm to retire, none of their children wanted the property, and they made the difficult decision to sell. They thoughtfully considered all the various potential buyers, not wanting the farm to fall into irresponsible hands, and believed they had passed it on to someone who would be a good steward of what they had worked so hard to preserve. They were shocked and grieved when the land was quickly sold again to a less responsible farmer who bulldozed all the trees in order to maximize the land he could put to seed. The family feels that careful work of generations is being rapidly undone and that the "mining of the soil" they had stewarded is a desecration of what is sacred.

One of the leaders of the agrarian movement is Wendell Berry, who farms in the Appalachian mountains of Kentucky. His land is sloping and therefore vulnerable to erosion. It is partly wooded and must be worked in small patches and plots rather than in the large fields that modern machinery is adapted for. He uses the term "kindly use" for the disciplined application of local knowledge to the challenges of farming specific plots of land:

> Kindly use is a concept that of necessity broadens, becoming more complex and diverse, as it approaches action. The land is too various in its kinds, climates, conditions, declivities, aspects, and histories to conform to any generalized understanding or to prosper under generalized treatment.... Kindly use depends upon intimate knowledge, the most sensitive responsiveness and responsibility.[18]

When the earth is viewed as sacred, intimate local knowledge becomes much more important, not only with respect to land use but for the wise stewardship of fisheries and other natural systems. But a global economy that treats people (especially farmers and fishers) as replaceable and interchangeable labour, and that deals with land and ecosystems in abstract, reductionist terms devalues such local knowledge, which is then lost.

Kindly use, it seems to me, is what transforms stewardship into a social practice for sustainable communities. Kindly use is an essential ingredient of wise stewardship in our time, a stewardship dependent on intimate local knowledge of land and ecosystems. Separated from such intimate knowledge and an ethic of kindly use, stewardship can easily become an abstract concept that only slightly restrains the temptation to abuse our power over the natural world.[19]

The Image of God

A steward is in charge of what is given to him/her, and has authority over it. Stewardship is the practice of the wise and judicious use of power in relation to other people and other creatures. The steward therefore has a special role and responsibility. The biblical story of creation speaks about that special role when it says that humans are created "in God's image," and given "dominion" over the rest of creation.

The image of God is an important theme in theological tradition and there has been much ink spilled over what it represents. Many theologians assume that the image of God is an attribute (like the ability to reason) that humans possess by the fact of being human. This way of understanding human nature nearly always contrasts the image of God with our physical or animal nature. It also tends to marginalize those who are seen stereotypically as less rational, such as the developmentally disabled, women, and children.

Douglas John Hall points out that a long-standing way of understanding this theme is to see the image of God as a pattern of life to aspire to. In this understanding the essential human vocation is "to image God." Just as a mirror only bears the image of the sun when turned toward it, so humans only image God when we reflect God in the way we live.

Dominion, the word from the biblical creation story, is defined by the character of the *dominus* (Lord). In Christian terms, the human vocation is to reflect the image of the God made known in Jesus Christ, whose dominion was exercised through sacrificial service. Humans have a special role in the creation, but that role must be guided by the example of Christ "who did not count equality with God a thing to be grasped, but emptied himself..." (Philippians 2:6–7). This self-emptying sacrifice is not an end in itself, however. Jesus' life, death, and resurrection were "for us." He "lay down his life for his friends." His sacrifice is in service of life: "I came that they might have life, and have it more abundantly." God's dominion over the world is for the sake of that world.

The agrarian concept of kindly use strikes me as entirely consistent with the kind of dominion Hall articulates. If the human call to live in the image of God is to mirror the divine glory that spends itself in love, then a kindly use that is responsive to the needs of the land and its creatures will empty itself of any desire to dominate. Such a practice of stewardship will approach natural systems with restraint and reverential attentiveness. It will not only speak of the earth as sacred, but will engage in practices that treat it as sacred.

Chapter Seven
PRACTICING REVERENCE

There are two ways to live:

you can live as if nothing is a miracle;

you can live as if everything is a miracle.

Albert Einstein

Ritual and Prayer

There are many ways to practice reverence, from the simple grace around a meal table to the elaborate centuries-old rituals of the Orthodox liturgy, from the thanksgiving of an aboriginal hunter for the life of an animal to the chant of a Tibetan monk. In my own Christian tradition, prayer may take the form of adoring praise, thanksgiving, confession, lament, supplication (our prayers for ourselves), or intercession (our prayers for others). I want to highlight the ways that prayer and worship support sustainable communities by nurturing alternatives to the dominant economic and technocratic practices. Such practices, done well, transform the character of the individuals and communities that perform them and nurture sustainable relationships with the rest of creation. Done poorly, they can reinforce unsustainable and unjust practices.

Human cultures develop and pass on a sense of the meaning of their lives through worship and ritual practices. These practices establish order and offer a sacred canopy within which life and its challenges can be met with confidence and hope. Tom Driver points out that ritual is essential to movements of social change. Ideas alone cannot bring about social change, because in order to move from theory to reality, they need to be enacted. Nor can political methods alone create a more just condition, because they are too compromised by the struggle for power and do not have the moral power of rituals to appeal to our highest values. Ritual is the necessary intermediate step between the ideal vision and the political reality.[1]

According to Driver, ritual practices support alternative communities in three different ways: by expressing alternative possibilities, by giving participants an experience of those alternatives, and by drawing on divine power to confront the established power of economic and political systems that are resistant to change.[2] It is worth exploring each of those points in more detail.

Firstly, dominant systems present themselves as natural, inevitable, or godly. They have "ideological power," or the ability to shape the ideas people have about the world. Technocratic science and abstract economics powerfully manipulate what we believe by obscuring both non-manipulative ways of seeing the world, and non-monetary values. Dominant systems wield ideological power that prevents people from recognizing or seeking alternatives. But ritual practices publicly express the possibility that life can be different. Ritual practices imagine the world as God desires it to be. For example, for Jews, the Passover ritual not only re-enacts the story of their liberation from slavery, it also exposes oppression in the present as something that should be resisted rather than assumed.

Prayers of thanksgiving and praise acknowledge a sense of the natural world as the "theatre of God's glory."[3] Prayers of confession say out loud that we live in ways that are not as God wants them to be. Christian sacraments like Holy Communion and baptism express God's grace through the common elements of water, wine, and bread, and expose a sacred dimension to eating and community life that is obscured by dominant world views. Ritual practices make it possible for people to imagine and seek alternative patterns of living. They serve as the bugle call rallying people for the struggle.[4]

Secondly, ritual practices invite participants into an experience of the different reality.[5] Ritual practices fuse the visionary and the actual, involving us, in Gandhi's words, in being the change we want to see in the world.

Voluntarily making an offering to support the mission of the faith community gives people an experience of a different way of relating economically to each other; they experience a community that is supported entirely by acts of unrewarded generosity.

In providing this alternative experience, ritual practices allow us to shift our focus to what we are struggling for and striving toward. The danger of focusing on what we are opposing is that we become fixated on the negative. "Whoever fights monsters," warned Frederick Nietzsche, "should see to it that in the process he does not become a monster."[6]

Third, ritual practices evoke moral and spiritual power as an alternative to the power of oppressive and destructive systems. "Not all power is physical and material," notes Tom Driver.[7] And it is the spiritual or ideological power of economic and technocratic systems that is the most intractable and resistant. Once the mystique of ideology is penetrated, oppressive systems change quite quickly, as we saw with the fall of the Berlin Wall, the end of apartheid in South Africa, and the fall of President Mubarak in Egypt. Up until the point when that kind of change occurs, ritual practices sustain alternative communities with the hope that there are powers at work in the world which are greater than even the most intractable systems.

The regular worship practices of religious communities sustain traditions of resistance to dominant practices in ways that may not always be fully realized by the participants. At some point however, those practices may burst forth beyond their safe and expected settings and engage dominant practices in new and unexpected ways.

The worship and ritual practices of black churches in the United States and South Africa had sustained an alternative to white racism for generations, but when the time was right, spirituals, songs, and prayers joined with ritual protest to challenge dominant practices with spiritual and moral power.[8] Through worshipful acts, the people confronted the power of violence with the faith that "we shall overcome one day." That faith was vindicated.

In the same way, the ritual protests of Greenpeace and other environmental groups take reverence for creation into the public sphere. In doing so, they have been surprisingly effective at drawing public attention, confronting dominant attitudes, and inviting people and systems to change. They might be more effective if there was a closer relationship between such groups and worshipping communities.

Praise

The rabbis tell a story about the creation of the world: After five days of creation, the Creator asked an angel whether anything was still missing. The angel answered that everything was perfect. It was, after all, God's handiwork. "Yet perhaps," the angel mused, "perhaps one thing could make this already perfect world yet more perfect: speech, to praise its perfection." And so God created the human creature, in order that the human capacity for speech might give rise to praise and thanksgiving.[9]

Of all the accounts of what it means for humans to live a good life, this one strikes me as the one most undervalued in the modern world, and perhaps the one most helpful in reclaiming our role as good citizens of the earth. That we were made to praise the Maker means that life can be fulfilled in each moment. We can praise whether our lives are short or long, impoverished or prosperous; with praise we can accomplish what we were made to do.

A common theme in Christian and Jewish theology is that part of the human vocation is to speak on behalf of non-human creation. As Jürgen Moltmann puts it, "Through human beings the sun and moon also glorify the Creator. Through human beings plants and animals also glorify the Creator...through him the cosmos sings before its Creator the eternal song of creation."[10]

That theme is balanced in some traditions with a belief that other creatures also offer praise, and may even serve to represent human beings.[11] Who is to say, for example, that the songs of birds and whales are not expressions of joy, delight, and praise? How could we rule out the possibility that the play of whales is not also a bodily expression of delight, joy, and thanksgiving? Certainly the biblical Psalms often suggest that the rest of creation is capable of praise: "Everything that breathes" praises God (Psalm 150:6, NRSV), and "the heavens tell of the glory of God" (Psalm 19:1, NLT).

Saint Francis of Assisi famously preached to the birds and called on all creatures to praise God. The Canticle of the Sun attributed to him has been translated into English by William Draper and sung as the popular hymn, "All Creatures of Our God and King."[12]

The hymn and the canticle are ambiguous: do they imply that the sun, moon, and other creatures are already praising God in their own ways, or that they need to begin to do so? In calling on all creatures to "lift up your voice and with us sing" the hymn implies that human praise is primary, and other creatures can sing along. It is cast in the imperative mood; it is a command or instruction to other creatures to praise God, implying that they are not already doing so.

The possibility that other creatures need to be coaxed into praise echoes the view of some theologians that non-human creation has "fallen" and no longer reflects the Creator's intent. In this view, creation cannot be equated with "nature" and the "natural world," because nature as we know it is disordered. In this view, Francis' canticle may be a call to a disordered creation to change and live out its true destiny in a right relationship of joy and praise to the Creator.

The possibility that other creatures may themselves offer praise echoes the view of other theologians that only the human component of creation has fallen and that non-human creation continues to be rightly related to the Creator through an ongoing chorus of praise. A modern hymn expresses unambiguously this view that the whole of creation is involved in a chorus of praise:

It's a song of praise to the Maker,
the thrush sings high in the tree.
It's a song of praise to the Maker,
the gray whale sings in the sea,
    And by the Spirit you and I
    can join our voice to the holy cry
    and sing, sing, sing to the Maker too.

It's the chorus of all creation;
it's sung by all living things.
It's the chorus of all creation;
a song the universe sings,
    And by the Spirit you and I
    can join our voice to the holy cry
    and sing, sing, sing to the Maker too.[13]

That hymn reverses the assumption made in "All Creatures of Our God and King." that other creatures join the human chorus. Here it is humans who can, by the Spirit, join other creatures who are continually, each in its own way, offering their praise.

My own view is that human sinfulness cannot help but affect the rest of creation. We are all bound together in relationship, for good or ill. But just as human sinfulness distorts our praise but does not silence it, so the human corruption of God's creation need not be seen as silencing the praise of other creatures.

Regardless of the position one takes on the theological question of whether the rest of creation is fallen or not, these hymns and prayers correct the common assumption that only humans are related to God. Humans are part of a cosmic choir where humans and nonhumans support one another in harmonies of gratitude and praise.

Lament

A lament is an expression of grief, sadness, anger, and regret. I think the communal prayer of lament has a neglected but important role to play in the ritual practices of sustainable communities; individual laments express personal grief, as in the African-American spiritual "Nobody Knows the Trouble I've Seen," and communal laments express shared grief and loss. Expressions of loss from the destruction of ecosystems have been an important part of the environmental movement from the very beginning. Many scientists have supplemented their factual descriptions and analysis of environmental destruction with accounts of their personal feelings of loss and grief: Aldo Leopold's description of the dying wolf and Joan Kleypas' account of her attack of nausea are two examples.

Recordings of whale songs gave the anti-whaling movement enormous impetus. For people who knew about the massive slaughter of whales, hearing those songs was like hearing them sing their own funeral dirges. The whale songs were felt as powerful, non-verbal expressions of grief.

Putting words to our situation of environmental peril acknowledges that we are violating important moral lines. Putting these words into the emotional language of lament helps the moral dimension of the destruction become visible. An economic and industrial system that treats all creation as a resource for human consumption sees environmental suffering and destruction as normal and natural. Lament exposes it as one alternative among others, a choice to be brought into consciousness and resisted.

In visiting the site of a Kentucky coal mine, Wendell Berry offered the following lament:

[S]tanding there in the very presence of it, one feels one's comprehension falling short of the magnitude of its immorality. One is surrounded by death and ugliness and silence as of the end of the world. After my first trip to this place I think I was most impressed by the extent of the destruction, and its speed; what most impresses me now is its permanence.... Standing and looking down on that mangled land, one feels aching in one's bones the sense that it will be in a place such as this – a place of titanic disorder and violence, which the rhetoric of political fantasy has obstructed from official eyesight – that the balance will finally be overcast and the world tilted

> irrevocably toward its death.... Since I left Hard-
> burly I have been unable to escape the sense that
> I have been to the top of the mountain, and that
> I have looked over and seen, not the promised
> land vouchsafed to a chosen people, but a land of
> violence and sterility prepared and set aside for
> the damned.[14]

Some people would look on such a site and see in it the
strange beauty of money, prosperity, and economic opportunity. To describe it as a foretaste of hell is to see
it differently from the dominant economic and technocratic view. And in seeing it differently, we can envision
alternatives.

Canadian singer/songwriter Bruce Cockburn laments the destruction of rainforests and the indigenous
peoples who have inhabited them for thousands of years
in his 1998 song, "If a Tree Falls in a Forest."[15]

> What kind of currency grows in these new deserts,
> These brand new flood plains?
> If a tree falls in the forest does anybody hear?
> If a tree falls in the forest does anybody hear?
> Anybody hear the forest fall?
>
> Cut and move on
> Cut and move on
> Take out trees
> Take out wildlife at a rate of species every single day
> Take out people who've lived with this for 100,000
>   years...

Cockburn's lyrics alone do not do justice to his vocal
performance, with its overtones of bewilderment, an-

guish, and anger. This song expresses both grief and an imperative to resist relentless deforestation. And it draws on indigenous spirituality to acknowledge that rainforest destruction and the extinction of species are spiritual issues: the logging industry is a "busy monster eating dark holes in the spirit world / where wild things have to go / to disappear / forever."

Margaret Atwood's novel *Year of the Flood* is a fictionalized account of an eco-religious community called God's Gardeners who live in a time of widespread ecological degradation. The book opens with a hymn of lament sung by the Gardeners:

Who is it tends the Garden,
The Garden oh so green?

'Twas once the finest Garden
That ever has been seen.

And in it God's dear Creatures
Did swim and fly and play;

But then came greedy Spoilers,
And killed them all away.

And all the Trees that flourished
And gave us wholesome fruit,

By waves of sand are buried,
Both leaf and branch and root.

And all the shining Water
Is turned to slime and mire,

And all the feathered Birds so bright
Have ceased their joyful choir.

Oh Garden, oh my Garden,
I'll mourn forevermore.

Until the Gardeners arise,
And you to Life restore.

Atwood's hymn is strongly ironic, with its overly romantic vision of nature, its simplistic ascription of blame for environmental destruction on the greedy, and its confidence in the capacity of the Gardeners to restore what has been lost. Still, by naming and mourning the destruction which has been experienced, the hymn evokes a long tradition of lament in the psalms, hymns, and prayers of worshipping communities. Such laments address the sacred and invoke a compassionate God who cares passionately about creation and who listens to such cries. And so, laments evoke not only a sense of grief for what is lost, but also reverence for what survives.

Lament as Prayer

The biblical laments are prayers that emerge from the depths of human experience, from times of life-threatening illness, death, persecution, torment – from suffering of all kinds. More than half of the Psalms are laments, as are large sections of the book of Job, and the entire book of Lamentations. While most are individual laments expressing grief over illness and persecution, many are responses to shared difficulties. These shared difficulties are often environmental stresses, as summarized in the prayer King Solomon is reported to

have offered at the dedication of the first temple in Jerusalem: "If the skies are shut up and there is no rain... If
there is a famine in the land, or plagues, or crop disease,
or attacks of locusts or caterpillars, or if your people's
enemies are in the land besieging their towns – whatever the trouble is – and if your people offer a prayer
concerning their troubles or sorrow, raising their hands
toward this Temple, then hear from heaven where you
live, and forgive" (1 Kings 8:35–39 NLT).

The biblical laments often assume that the trouble
facing the people is a symptom of a deeper, spiritual
problem, some estrangement between God and God's
people which needs to be put right. Sometimes there
is a sense that the sinning of God's people needs to be
addressed both through forgiveness on God's part and
renewed obedience on the part of the people. In our individualistic society, this sense of communal responsibility may seem foreign. But as we confront environmental
challenges, the practice of lament helpfully combines
grief for what is lost with a confession of the ways in
which we participate (often passively) in practices that
degrade natural systems. The following prayer of confession explicitly acknowledges this sense of communal
responsibility for the degradation of natural systems.

> We remember and confess how we have poisoned
>   and polluted the rivers in our garden planet.
> **Christ, crucified on a tree, hear our cry.**
> We regret that we have forgotten Earth and
>   treated this garden planet as a beast to be
>   tamed and as a place to be ruled.
> **Christ, the hope of all creation, we lament our**
>   **failings.**

> We have polluted our rivers with poisons, treat-
> ed our streams as waste dumps, drained our
> wetlands of life, and turned living waters
> into deathtraps.
> **Christ, the source of all life, we are sorry.**
> **We are sorry.** [16]

Such responsibility is not equally shared. The wealthy developed nations, for example, have contributed the most to rising levels of carbon dioxide in the atmosphere, but the most serious effects of climate change will be felt by indigenous people in the North and impoverished people in the developing world. These relatively powerless people might well protest their innocence, as biblical laments sometimes also do.[17] Such protestations of innocence reflect the reality that the human suffering resulting from the degradation of natural systems is often experienced by those who have contributed little to the problem.

Whatever the perceived cause, the prayer of lament trusts that suffering concerns God. This trust, however, is not naïve faith that avoids the reality that life is often unfair. Even in turning to God, it pounds on the gates of heaven with outrage at how God's world is not just and fair and God has failed to act to uphold justice. This is clear in the famous lament from Psalm 22: "My God, my God, why have you forsaken me?" That cry of dereliction echoes through the ages in the cries of those who experience suffering, who feel forsaken by the one the faith community confesses as the friend of the poor and the defender of the defenceless.

When Jesus uttered his own anguished cry from the cross using those ancient words, a paradox entered the practice of lament: God experiences God-forsakenness. Because Christians view Jesus as both human and divine, his sense of God-forsakenness becomes a means through which God addresses the suffering of creation by participating in it. God is revealed as present in and with the suffering, and as being served by acts of compassion toward the "least of these" (Matthew 25:40, 45). This sense of God suffering with the suffering is well expressed in a modern hymn called "God Weeps."

> God weeps at love withheld, at strength misused,
> at children's innocence abused,
> and till we change the way we love, God weeps.

> God cries at hungry mouths, at running sores,
> at creatures dying without cause,
> and till we change the way we care, God cries. [18]

The divine is no longer seen as the capricious power behind history, acting in and through kings and empire. Rather, the Christian story makes the astounding claim that the divine begins life as a homeless refugee and ends as a victim of brutal execution. The claim that God is revealed in the life of this person utterly transforms the character of lament. Lament is no longer a cry to a remote God whose attention needs to be drawn to the suffering of his people: it becomes a conversation with one who shares intimately in the experience of suffering and knows it from personal experience.

Reflection on the life of Jesus has another influence on lament: because Jesus experienced suffering at the hands of agents of the Roman Empire and its Judean collaborators, the cause of suffering is demystified. Suffering is no longer solely the mysterious action of a God who must be appeased or placated, but the result of discernible forces that can be analyzed and addressed. The cause of suffering is redirected to these creaturely forces, and prayer becomes an appeal to God as an ally in the struggle against suffering. And so, as the writers of the New Testament reflect on the suffering they and others experience, they increasingly become concerned with addressing the "powers" – not just powerful individuals and groups, but the systems of language, ideas, and communal practices which legitimate them. Today, the phrase "the powers that be" describes these forces.

Lament in the Christian tradition is a practice that names problems, articulates our grief over them, looks for their causes (including confessing our own complicity in them when appropriate), and calls on divine power for aid, confident that God shares our grief. Such laments address the sacred and invoke a compassionate God who hears such cries. And because they are confident that God cares, they invite us into an attitude of reverence before that for which God weeps.

Lament, praise, and other practices of public ritual can sustain reverence for God's creation. They can also sustain trust that our faithful action towards moral ends can challenge and overturn even the most intractable of oppressive systems. Finally, when they are taken out of the safety of sanctuaries into the public realm, they can challenge dominant patterns of thinking and acting with moral and spiritual power.

Chapter Eight
NO FATE:
THE PRACTICES
OF HOPE

Hope has two lovely daughters, anger and courage:
anger, so that what must not be, shall not be;
courage, so that what must be, shall be."

Augustine of Hippo[1] (354–430 CE)

The title of this chapter is from the science-fiction movie *Terminator 2: Judgement Day*. In the film, powerful robot assassins ("terminators") from a post-apocalyptic future travel back in time to either help or hinder human survival. The theme of the movie is expressed in a cluster of short sentences: "No fate. The future's not set. There's no fate but what we make ourselves."[2] The suspense arises from the question of which future will actually emerge from the many possibilities. Nuclear or environmental apocalypses are possibilities. There are others. But what is clear is that the future depends on the choices made in the present.

I agree that human action is a significant factor affecting our future. I do not agree that it is the only significant factor. I believe it is complemented by a mysterious power at work, to which some give the inadequate name of God. We are so seduced by the power of our own abilities to predict and control that we lose sight of the reality that the universe is infinitely complex and resists our best efforts at prognostication. There are powers at work that may only be recognized in retrospect. History is surprising. Life is surprising. There is a mystery at work that cannot be controlled or predicted.

We live in the presence of both profound evil and marvellous goodness. Evil and goodness are not easy to separate – like yin and yang they interpenetrate each other. Our choices are often tragic ones between shades of grey. Even so, different choices lead to significantly different outcomes, and some choices are demonstrably better than others. Our actions need to be guided by a thoroughly realistic view of human nature that is informed by a deep awareness of human sin and finitude.

Different perspectives on the future have different ethical implications. If we see the future as predestined, irrespective of our action, then we will see no point to any particular effort or sacrifice to make that future better. If we see the earth as doomed to destruction, then efforts to halt the destruction are irrelevant. If we reject ecological concerns as mistaken pessimism in the face of glorious progress, then efforts to rethink the direction of our economic and political trends will be scoffed at and bitterly opposed. But if we see the possibilities for both evil and good to emerge from our present situation, then we must imagine and live out the best possible future. If we see that we have an important part to play in shaping an open future, then we recognize that our actions are vitally important.

The German theologian Jürgen Moltmann pointed out that if we knew for certain that a nuclear or environmental catastrophe was going to happen, we could do nothing. On the other hand, if we knew for certain that the future would steadily improve we would need to do nothing. But because such a catastrophe is possible, but not certain, our actions become important and our choices critical. Because the future is open, we must act as if the future depends entirely on our choices, and at the same time trust that God is faithful and is at work in us and others.[3]

Christian hope is not passive. Jesus sent his disciples out to heal and teach in his name. In doing so, he invited them to participate in the new community God was shaping. This is participatory hope.[4] Jesus taught that Spirit works in countless ways, few of which are independent of human initiative. As Martin Luther King, Jr. once said, "Human progress never rolls in on wheels of inevitability; it comes through the tireless efforts of people willing to be co-workers with God."[5] Or as Don Tapscott puts it, "The future is not something to be predicted, but something to be achieved."[6]

This chapter explores practices that sustain a realistic but hopeful spirit. The challenges facing us are prodigious, and we do not know precisely whether or how we can overcome them. The solutions to our problems are not obvious, and it is important to think carefully about them while drawing on every source of wisdom at our disposal.

I want to explore the practices that support communities as they take hopeful action towards a more sustainable way of life. First, I look at the work of shaping anticipatory communities, communities that bear witness to a better future by living as if that future were already present. Then I explore the practice of keeping Sabbath in Jewish and Christian communities, which invites us into a space of worship and rest where space for enjoying and anticipating God's creation is preserved. Finally, I conclude with a reflection on the importance of humour, which helps us not to take either our problems or ourselves too seriously. None of these practices encourages wishful thinking or passive hope. These practices are for people who know the way ahead will be difficult and challenging at every turn. These practices are for those who know they need the strength of tested spiritual traditions to sustain hope and joy in difficult times.

Anticipatory Community

Because our culture is dominated by the assumption that humans can and should be in control, the sheer scale of environmental degradation results in particularly troubling attitudes. We are caught between two approaches, neither of which seems adequate to the challenge. On the one hand, the problem is overwhelming in scale. What can any single person or group of people do to address such a difficult challenge? When a space shuttle flight burns more fossil fuel than I will use in my lifetime, what difference does it make whether I drive an SUV or ride a bike?

On the other hand, we rely so heavily on our systems of government, economy, and technology that even when we have good evidence that they are failing to meet a crisis it is easier to turn a blind eye and trust that some expert, somewhere, is figuring it out. We end up placing our trust in the very patterns of control and management that are characteristic of technocratic science and abstract economics. And so proposals for "sustainable" development and investment in "green" technology end up being not very different from old-style development and old technology.

These two ways of thinking about the problem lead to a kind of paralysis. Either we feel we are powerless because there is nothing we can do, or we are complacent because we believe there is nothing we need to do. Both those approaches, however, appeal to arguments from consequences. They assume that the way to decide the right thing to do is to calculate the most effective route to meet the goal of sustainability. Our powerlessness arises out of a sense that no action on our part will contribute any measurable progress towards our goal. Our complacency arises from a calculation that there is nothing we need to do to meet the same goal.

We need to go further and recognize that a focus on consequences falls into the modern hubris of management and control, described in the serpent's original temptation to become like God (Genesis 3:5). In Laura Yordy's words:

This enthrallment with effectiveness pervades our society, but it has particular ramifications for Christian life. Some attention to effectiveness is, of course, part of Christian prudence; we want our deeds of charity and justice to realize our intentions. Too much focus on consequences, however, feeds into the notion that humans are God's managers rather than God's creatures – that only human efforts hold any hope for the future.[7]

This book proposes that we take a different route and make our choices based on the kind of person we want to be and the kind of community we want to live in. If we focus on developing and living in communities of integrity, and shaping our lives by practices of hope, reverence, loyalty, neighbourliness, and stewardship, we might escape the powerlessness/complacency trap.

The Koinonia Farm in Americus, Georgia, is an example of such a community of integrity. *Koinonia* is a Greek word meaning "community" or "fellowship." Koinonia Farm was founded in 1942 by two Christian couples as a "demonstration plot for the Kingdom of God."[8] Clarence Jordan, who was the unofficial spiritual leader of the community, felt called to form a community that would consciously imitate the first Christian communities described in the New Testament book of Acts. Like the members of the early church, residents of Koinonia Farm would share possessions, pursue racial justice, act non-violently, and conserve the soil, "God's holy earth."[9]

In the time he had free from farm work, Clarence visited black and white churches, teaching and supporting the often poorly educated pastors. Eventually he wrote a series of books translating the New Testament into the language of the rural South. They are known as the Cotton Patch translations.

From the beginning, Koinonia was intended as a community that would resist the barriers of poverty and racism so prevalent in the rural South. When the community could afford to hire farm workers, black and white workers were paid equal wages and everyone ate at the same table. Members of the community reached out to black neighbours and established relationships of mutual support, seriously challenging the prevailing segregationist culture and leading to serious conflict with the Ku Klux Klan and the local White Citizen's Council. The members endured firebombs, bullets, KKK rallies, death threats, property damage, and boycotts of farm products. They were also expelled from local white churches. But they endured, and in enduring they served as a concrete example that a different way of living in community is possible.

Koinonia Farm gave rise to several innovative ministries. The most famous is Habitat for Humanity, which grew out of the efforts of the members of the community to provide practical help for poor neighbours who often lived in substandard housing.

Koinonia Farm sought to be a "demonstration plot" of God's Kingdom. This community of witness is an example of what Bruce Birch and Larry Rasmussen call an anticipatory community, one that seeks to model a better future. Such communities are communities of resistance to dominant patterns of behaviour. But they are not focused on what they resist. Rather their community life reflects what they hope for.

Another example of an anticipatory community developed during the Nazi regime in Germany, when the anti-Semitic German Christian movement co-opted the dominant state church.[10] A few people who rejected this development formed an alternative church known as the Confessing Church. German pastor and theologian Dietrich Bonhoeffer became the leader of the seminary of the Confessing Church, which went underground when the church was outlawed. The young men training for leadership lived and studied together and developed a rich community life. Bonhoeffer described that experience in his book *Life Together*, which shares some important insights about how to nurture and maintain alternative communities. Writing in a time of struggle and unrest Bonhoeffer believed that alternative communities need to embrace a double movement, a "journey inward, journey outward."[11]

The Inward and Outward Journeys

The inward journey is the life of disciplined Christian community. Members of such communities delve deeply into the arcane disciplines of prayer, lament, and community accountability. (These practices are referred to as arcane [or foreign] because they appear peculiar and eccentric to those who are outside of, or new to the community.) Through such disciplines, participants engage deeply with God and with each other. Bruce Birch and Larry Rasmussen describe the concept:

> Arcane discipline is not for everyone... It is for small groups of Christians who express their loyalty to Christ with one another in worship... It is not for the streets, for the posters, for the media, or for the masses. It is not bumper-sticker Christianity, slick-paper evangelism, drive-in worship, or American civil religion. It is demanding in its stipulations for membership and participation,

and regular in its practice of disciplines. It asks sacrifice...[12]

Many in our consumer age approach faith communities like shoppers in supermarkets, picking what they want and leaving the rest. They judge the practices of faith communities according to their current preferences. Alternatively, those who practice arcane disciplines resist consumer temptations and open themselves to being changed by transformational practices. They allow arcane practices to change their preferences and transform their desires. Anticipatory communities are held together by shared practices that are intended to be transformational for the participants.

People in anticipatory communities that are seeking to be sustainable will find ways to support each other while questioning their lifestyles, experimenting with new rituals and technologies, and growing into deeper integrity. They will find ways to celebrate the common and routine, to live "as if" the barriers between rich and poor, human and non-human have already been transcended, and to live in a spirit of joyful austerity.

The journey outward is the effort to serve the common good, to carry the wisdom and insight gained through arcane practices beyond the boundaries of that community. Sustainable communities strive to serve and empower the vulnerable members of society. They seek to share what they have learned about sustainable living. They invite others to learn from their experience, and they challenge those who continue to live in destructive ways. They seek to bear witness to the community's hopeful vision of the future in their dialogue with those who are not part of the community.

The inward and outward journeys must stand in tension with each other. Without the outward journey, the inward journey becomes self-absorbed, sectarian, pious, and self-righteous. Without the inward journey, however, the outward journey becomes subject to burn-out and easy identification with fashionable causes.

The Opportunity

An anticipatory community has the opportunity to experiment with a new pattern of life, working in trial and error fashion over a protracted period of time. Birch and Rasmussen point out that such communities need the "nerve of failure," a willingness to take risks, make mistakes, and appear foolish. They will be "sacred strangers in secular society," and their existence constitutes a challenge and offers an alternative to the rest of society.

Laura Yordy offers a number of very practical suggestions about how even small churches can become such communities of witness. Pointing out the harmful agricultural practices and poor working conditions of farm workers involved in the production of wine and grape juice commonly used in Christian worship for Holy Communion, she proposes searching out wine and juice that is produced ethically. "Even if churches cannot locate organic, fair-trade wine, the act of asking the questions may eventually encourage wineries to improve their production methods. Similar questions could be asked about the way that Communion bread is produced. This kind of work, inefficient, tedious, and without satisfying results, is the work of witnessing to the peace and justice of the Kingdom of God – the work of discipleship."[13] Because the celebration of Holy Communion is an arcane discipline at the heart of Christian worship, it is crucial that the bread and wine used in them are not the "toxic fruit" of harmful agricultural methods.

This should not be taken as a yearning for moral purity, as if there were some way of sanitizing Eucharist beyond all human sin, or as if the "right" offerings secure a higher level of faithfulness. Rather, for the church to be a living sign of the Kingdom of God, it must continually strive to demonstrate the possibilities of justice, peace, and abundance.[14]

In the modern economy it is nearly impossible to avoid participating in food production systems that exploit human workers, but wherever possible we should purchase and use products that are produced justly. Yordy suggests using fair trade products and minimizing the use of meat at church meals (or at least using meat from local suppliers where the conditions under which the animal was raised and slaughtered can be verified). She also proposes that church properties be landscaped with native species and maintained with a minimum of fertilizer and pesticides. Similarly, Norman Wirzba argues that if churches, synagogues, and mosques converted their lawns and parking lots into vegetable and flower gardens, which then became inspiration for local food economies, the impact could be far-reaching.

> Ecologists have taught us that all life forms one unfathomably complex and interconnected whole. Each part matters and every part, however minutely, influences the rest. This is good news because it means that if we get something as basic and far-reaching as eating right, so much other good will follow... Imagine if all followers of the gardening God became advocates and supporters of public policies and economic practices that made the healing of each place a top priority.[15]

Such suggestions may seem minor compared to the ecological challenges we face, and they should not be seen
as alternatives to addressing the economic, political, and
technological challenges we have explored, but they are
small ways in which faith communities can anticipate
a sustainable society and bear witness to an alternative
future.

Practicing Sabbath

One of the ancient arcane disciplines by which communities can anticipate a sustainable future is through some
form of Sabbath observance. In the Jewish and Christian communities, the practice of Sabbath observance is
a ritual that proclaims, enacts, and evokes divine power
on behalf of the social and ecological harmony that sustainable communities desire.

The Sabbath is the seventh day of the week, and in
Jewish tradition it is a day to refrain from work in order to celebrate God's gifts. Stopping all non-essential
activity gives us space to become aware of how we may
define ourselves by our work and achievements. Sabbath
"is a central affirmation to Israel about the character of
life and land as gift. It is the institutional reminder to Israel that cessation from frantic activity will not cause the
world to disintegrate or society to collapse. Sabbath sets
a boundary to our best, most intense efforts to manage
life and organize land for our security and well-being."[16]

The Sabbath is not a day of solemnity or fasting,
but a day to enjoy God's creation, celebrate God's gifts,
and take "delight in the Lord" (Isaiah 58:13–14). Ob-
servant Jews are encouraged to feast and enjoy spend-
ing time with family and friends. It is a day to enjoy
bodily pleasures. Married couples are encouraged to

make a special point of making love on the Sabbath day. By setting aside the compulsion to work and produce, Sabbath observance encourages practitioners to receive land and other natural systems as gifts to be enjoyed and celebrated rather than as resources to be consumed. The regular practice of stopping work to rest and enjoy God's gifts also helps release those who practice it from the anxiety that feeds lifestyles of excess consumption.

Sabbath observance is the fourth of the Ten Commandments in both versions of those Commandments (Exodus 20:8–11 and Deuteronomy 5:12–15). The commandment itself is nearly identical in the two versions: "Remember the Sabbath day, and keep it holy. Six days you shall labor and do all your work. But the seventh day is a Sabbath to the Lord your God; you shall not do any work – you, your son or your daughter, your male or female slave, your livestock, or the alien resident in your towns." It is clear that Sabbath is a communal practice in which everyone and everything is allowed to rest (Exodus 23:12). This insistence that working animals were to be allowed to rest is among the first examples of a moral restraint on the use of animals. The closely related concept of the Sabbatical Year insists that the land too should be allowed to rest by lying fallow every seven years. Together, Sabbath and Sabbatical Year express the conviction that humans, land, animals, and all other creatures are bound together in an earth community that is able to rest together. The Sabbath is therefore intended to be an experience of participation in creation and an experience of harmony with creation.

The Hebrew word used for rest in Genesis and Exodus is *menuha*, a word that carries a rich constellation of meaning. As the Jewish theologian Abraham Joshua Heschel says,

To the Biblical mind, *menuha* is the same as happiness and stillness, as peace and harmony. The word with which Job described the state after life he was longing for is derived from the same root as *menuha*. It is the state wherein man lies still, wherein the wicked cease from troubling and the weary are at rest. It is the state in which there is no strife and no fighting, no fear and no distrust. The essence of good life is *menuha*. "The Lord is my shepherd, I shall not want, He maketh me lie down in green pastures; He leadeth me beside still waters" (the waters of *menuhot*). In later times *menuha* became a synonym for the life in the world to come, for eternal life.[17]

The day of rest, therefore, looks back to the original creation that God called "very good" and forward to the fulfillment and consummation of creation. Sabbath rest, in the words of David Holmes, "is meant to be a taste of this eternal life, one to which all creation is invited – slaves and free, animal and human, Israelite and foreigner."[18]

Practices can be done poorly, or with excellence. Poor Sabbath practice focuses primarily on the negative restrictions rather than on the positive intention. In his teachings about how to practice Sabbath well, Jesus was often in conflict with those who practiced it poorly.

Christian interpretations of the teachings of Jesus have often read his disputes with Pharisees over Sabbath observance as an annulment of the requirements of the Sabbath traditions. But recent Jewish-Christian dialogue about this issue has shown that much of Jesus' teaching was in strong continuity with other leading Jewish thinkers of the time. Jesus appealed to traditional Jewish rabbinic teachings that work could be performed on the Sabbath to save oneself from danger, to help others in danger, for ritual reasons, or to assist animals. The aphorism "the Sabbath was made for humanity, not humanity for the Sabbath" (Mark 2:27) was also part of rabbinic teaching.

One significant point (and one of controversy) is that Jesus saw his healing activity as being especially suitable for the Sabbath: "Ought not this woman, a daughter of Abraham whom Satan has bound for eighteen long years, be set free on the Sabbath day?" (Luke 13:16) Jesus is emphasizing the positive meaning of the Sabbath as a day for freedom and liberation. He was teaching that freedom can be found through a fulfillment of Sabbath in God's Kingdom: "Do not think that I have come to abolish the law or the prophets; I have come not to abolish but to fulfill" (Matthew 5:17).

Jesus had initiated a renewal movement within Judaism, and all of his earliest followers were Jews. Within a generation of his death, however, the movement was made up largely of Gentiles (non-Jews). Under the influence of Paul's letter to the Galatians, which insisted that Gentiles did not need to become Jews in order to be Christians, the specifically Jewish practice of Sabbath observance was not carried over into Christianity. Gentile Christians made the first day of the week the major day of worship because Jesus was raised from death on that day. But the movement called church[19] saw itself as the community of the resurrection, the Body of Christ, and therefore the seed of God's kingdom. The church saw itself as becoming what the Sabbath was in Israel: a foretaste of peace between humanity, nature, and God.

The Sabbath traditions emerged from Israel's history as landholders, and were designed in order to guide its stewardship of the land. Jesus' teaching, on the other hand, was addressed primarily to dispossessed peasant farmers and landless labourers, of whom he, as a carpenter, was one. The ethical issues they faced were different. As a result the specifically ecological dimensions of the Sabbath traditions are somewhat muted in Jesus' teaching. As the Christian movement made its transition from the rural society of Galilee to an urban movement, first in Jerusalem and later in cities around the Roman Empire, it is not surprising that the specifically agricultural and ecological dimensions of the Sabbath traditions played a subordinate role in Christian tradition.

In my own denomination, many people make an effort to observe Sunday as a day of rest, worship, and family time, although the form of that observance is largely left up to individual decision. Some people have little choice but to work on Sunday. As a minister, I work on Sundays and make a point of taking Mondays off, but my wife and children work on Mondays, so my days off are often spent in solitude. My experience is becoming increasingly common as service and retail industries operate seven days a week and sometimes twenty-four hours a day, with different family members having to work different shifts. Family time is increasingly fragmented, and community life is even more so. As a result, Sabbath observance is becoming less an activity that the community shares and more a personal lifestyle choice, which is not at all the same thing.

This situation is not entirely new, though. The early Christian movement included many slaves who had to work long, unpredictable hours, and who subsequently found participation in community worship and meals to be problematic. Paul's letters to the Corinthian church deal with some of the tensions within the community caused by the different social situations of the participants. He chastises those who fail to pay attention to the special challenges faced by some members, and encourages all community members to wait for those who are delayed by their responsibilities. By not doing so, he says, they humiliate other members of the community (1 Corinthians 11:18–34).

The concern for community that Paul models and encourages should encourage us to seek out solutions that express care and respect for the diverse membership of the communities we inhabit. Modern Sabbath observance will have to find its own rhythms.

Still, Sabbath observance in both Jewish and Christian communities can serve as a formative practice for sustainability. By making an effort to stop working and shopping for one day (whatever day that may be), people and communities remind one another that their lives are not defined primarily by consumer economics. They become more able to resist modern marketing methods and social pressures that highlight conspicuous consumption and frantic activity as markers of social status.

By resisting these trends, communities and their members proclaim the need for alternatives to our modern way of life, and demonstrate that alternatives are not only possible but joyful, life-giving, and desirable. Finally, they evoke divine power, not only in support of the practice, but in support of the work from which the practitioners of Sabbath refrain. By stopping even our most urgent work we acknowledge that we are not in control, and we do not need to be. We reject the modern temptation of total management and efficiency and learn to laugh, play, and turn over even the most pressing tasks to God. As the farmer-poet Wendell Berry puts it,

Harvest will fill the barn; for that
The hand must ache, the face must sweat.

And yet no leaf or grain is filled
By work of ours; the field is tilled
And left to grace. That we may reap,
Great work is done while we're asleep.

When we work well, a Sabbath mood
Rests on our day, and finds it good.[20]

Hope and Humour

I began this book with a joke because I believe that humour is an important ethical resource and a sign of the Spirit's activity in its own right, so I want to end the book on the same note.

Sigmund Freud observed that humour has a liberating quality that consists of "its refusal to be hurt by the arrows of reality or to be compelled to suffer. It insists that it is in fact impervious to wounds dealt by the outside world."[21]

Humour's ability to transcend troubling circumstances is one sign of the transcendence of God. Karl Barth, one of the great theologians of the 20th century, referred to theology as "a joyful science" precisely because of this transcendent quality in which faith, humour, and joy are linked.

W. O. Mitchell suggested something of this power of humour in a short story he wrote about a big city university professor who went to a small prairie town during World War II to do some field research on what the locals called "tall tales." The professor, however, referred to their tall tales as lies. He would go about town asking people to tell him their lies, and they would look at him befuddled. "Lies?! Folks around here are honest," they would say. "We don't tell lies." But every time someone told a tall tale, the professor would pull out his little notebook and start scribbling madly. Relations with the townsfolk generally deteriorated from there.

But right at the end of the story, the professor redeemed himself. He came up with a tall tale of his own, a real whopper, about an enormous grasshopper. This grasshopper was so big that when it landed near an airfield, the men pumped a hundred gallons of fuel into it before realizing it wasn't a plane. It was so big that it squashed a man to death when it landed in one town. It was so big that it spit tobacco juice and smeared an entire newly painted schoolhouse. It was so big that it laid an egg the size of a chicken coop. It was so big that bullets and buckshot bounced off its chitinous hide, and it only left when it developed some amorous feelings for a passing Lancaster bomber.

It turned out that the reason the professor was so interested in tall tales is that he saw them as expressions of hope in difficult times, as ways of making fun of the very things that most threatened the farmers' livelihoods. "Grasshoppers? You think these grasshoppers are big? You should have seen the one that landed over by Jackson's barn in '29. Now that was a grasshopper!"

"This is a hard country," the professor said. "There are grasshoppers that devour precious crops. There are drouth [sic], blizzards, loneliness. A man is a pretty small thing out on all this prairie. He is at the mercy of the elements... These men lie about the things that hurt them most. Their yarns are about the winters and how cold they are...the summers and how dry they are. In this country you get the deepest snow, the worst dust storms, the biggest hailstones... Rust and dust and hail and sawfly and cutworm and drouth are terrible things, but not half as frightening if they are made ridiculous. If a man can laugh at them he's won half the battle. When he exaggerates things he isn't lying really; it's a defense, the defense of exaggeration. He can either do that or squeal.... People in this country aren't squealers."[22]

Tall tales, in W. O. Mitchell's view, are a significant form of faith, a means of sustaining our hope in the midst of difficult and dangerous times. They allow us to laugh at the things we fear the most, not denying their power but mocking it, and claiming a hope that transcends it.

We need the hopeful and liberating quality of humour for the difficult and dangerous times ahead. We need to be able to laugh at our troubles and at ourselves. We need to learn not to take our problems or our solutions too seriously. We need to learn to try out new ways of living, much as children at play try out different roles and relationships. We have to learn that living the good life has little to do getting new practices right the first time and everything to do with accepting the risk of failure. We have to learn that struggles can draw us together and make possible a deeper and richer joy.

CONCLUSION

I do not understand my own actions.
For I do not do what I want,
* but I do the very thing I hate....*
I can will what is right, but I cannot do it.
For I do not do the good I want,
* but the evil I do not want is what I do.*

St. Paul[1]

When I was in my early twenties I spent three months living and working in the city of Linden in the South American country of Guyana. Tropical rain forest dominated the landscape outside the city for hundreds of kilometres. From the highway one could see tall trees dripping with vines, and thick vegetation growing at each level of the forest canopy. Birds and butterflies flitted from one tree to another. We city-dwellers were very aware of the forest that surrounded us.

However, the city of Linden was a blighted landscape, the baked red earth stripped of ground cover and hard as concrete. Linden's economy was based on bauxite mining, and mine tailings had been dumped into areas of pristine forest. The dead twisted trunks of once majestic trees still stood, but nothing else grew from the toxic ground. I remember feeling that the place was spooky, even in bright sunshine, as though haunted by the tormented ghosts of the former inhabitants. I had a sense that the practices of that mine were "eating dark holes in the spirit world."[2] Even today, more than three decades later, I deeply sense the desecration when I think about that area. I wonder what happened to all the plants, birds, animals, and other creatures that lived in that region when the tailings were dumped. How many species, uniquely adapted to that local habitat, are now extinct?

Bauxite is the raw material from which aluminum is made, so the pots and aluminum foil that I use in my kitchen may be the products of that mine. Unwittingly, I may have contributed to that haunted, blighted landscape. As I live in the modern global economy, I consume products that are mined, harvested, and produced in many different parts of the world. My consumption of these products contributes to deforestation in Brazil, dead zones off the coast of China, oil spills in the Gulf of Mexico, ocean acidification, climate change, and many, many other problems. Even though I am deeply concerned about the environment, I choose, although often vaguely or unconsciously, to participate in practices that contribute to serious environmental problems. But because those practices are social ones, and many people participate in them, as a single individual I am unable to change them.

When we drive a car, carry a cell phone, heat or cool our homes, buy clothes, or eat, we engage in patterns of economic life that are profoundly destructive. Despite our best intentions, we cause enormous damage and tremendous suffering. The words of the apostle Paul describe very accurately our experience of living in the modern world: "I do not do the good I want, but the evil I do not want is what I do."

I have a profound sense of moral responsibility for the impact my way of life is having. And as a father, I worry about the legacy I am leaving for future generations. The choices I make today will impact the way my children live when they retire in about forty years. Any grandchildren I have will inherit that world, as will my great-grandchildren and great-great-grandchildren. The more I learn about climate change, habitat loss, species extinction, and pollution, the more it terrifies me to think about the choices we are all making and the kind of world that future generations will live in. I worry that my descendants will never experience healthy forests and wetlands, but only the dead twisted trunks of once-lush ecosystems.

I suspect, however, that my descendants will live privileged lives compared to many in the world's impoverished countries. For them, environmental problems, even today, are matters of life and death, of whether people are able to drink clean water and produce enough food to feed themselves. Climate change, for example, is causing crop failures in areas as far-flung as Uganda and Guatemala.

When my children were small, we played a game called *Jenga*. We built a tower out of nearly identically shaped wooden blocks. Then we took turns removing wooden blocks from lower levels of the tower and adding them to the top. Tiny variations in the width and height of the blocks meant that some blocks were less critical to the structure of the tower than others. But as blocks were moved from lower to higher levels, the tower grew higher even as its foundation became less solid. At some point in the game, the tower became so unstable that even a slight movement sent it crashing to the ground. Our social systems, as they undermine the stability of the natural systems on which they are built even as they grow ever more complex, are like those unstable towers of wooden blocks.

In his book *Collapse*, Jared Diamond thoroughly documents how the undermining of ecosystems led to the collapse of some societies, both ancient and modern. The destruction of the environmental base led to increasing social tension, conflict over scarce resources, and dramatic declines in population.

In 2004 the Nobel Peace Prize was awarded to Wangari Maathai, the Kenyan leader of a movement dedicated to empowering women and combating deforestation. This announcement generated controversy among those who think of peace and security primarily in military terms. To award the Nobel Peace Prize to a woman best known for planting trees seemed frivolous. Wangari Maathai herself says that she was awarded the Nobel

Prize as a representative of a vast number of people and organizations who work on the linkages between environmental sustainability, poverty, human rights, and human security issues.

> The Norwegian Nobel Committee recognized that in order to have peace, countries need to manage the environment sustainably... and consciously promote equitable distribution of those resources.... It is probably not a coincidence that countries that have wide gaps between the rich and the poor, where inequities are glaring, where environment is destroyed, the poor are sacrificed and marginalized and the rich are greedy, corrupt and arrogant that it is also in those countries that insecurity, crime, conflicts and wars dominate the headlines. [3]

The reverse is also true: healthy environments and social justice reinforce and support each other and make for healthy, prosperous, and stable societies. Maathai's own work demonstrates how to go about building such societies. Planting a whole forest may seem daunting, but just as the journey of a thousand miles begins with a single step, so planting a forest begins with planting a single tree. Changing a society likewise begins by changing our hearts, one practice at a time.

As inspirited flesh and enfleshed spirits, we humans are profoundly dependent on the natural systems in which we are embedded. Our bodies depend on the clean water and healthy food that only healthy natural systems can provide. But our deepest joys and greatest pleasures also come from being in the body – enjoying good food and drink, lovemaking, and physical work. Video games are no substitute for athletic pursuits, and chat rooms are only a warm-up for the physical encounter. As bodily beings, we find our deepest joy in what engages us as whole beings: mind and heart, spirit and body. So I am convinced that finding more sustainable ways to live as part of the earth's natural systems will also lead to greater joy and happier lives.

In this book, I have explored some foundational practices that can point the way to happier, healthier lives and more sustainable communities. There are hundreds, even thousands of other practices that could be explored, but the religious, scientific, and economic practices identified here are basic to many others. In learning why our way of life is so destructive and what we have to do to change it, we have to grapple with these foundational practices and make the shift from consumer to sustainable society.

The shift from destructive to sustainable patterns of living is the great work of our time. In the ancient words of the Christian tradition, it is *metanoia* (repentance) and *conversio* (conversion), both of which mean literally to turn around and change direction. They are about more than just thinking differently, but living differently, even being different. While some associate these terms primarily with a specific kind of religious experience, I use them here in a broader sense to mean that broad turning described by Thomas Berry as "the transition from a period of human devastation of the Earth to a period when humans would be present to the planet in a mutually beneficial manner."[4]

I use the religious terms of repentance and conversion cautiously, for this is a transition that will transcend any particular religious, cultural, or national group. Each group will need to find ways to make that broad turn in its own way, and each group needs to find the resources to engage that turning in its own cultural and religious heritage. The value of the language of repentance and conversion, though, is that they make it clear that the turning needs to happen at a very deep level – the level of what we care about, appreciate, enjoy, and hope for – the level of character.

In their study of psychological and theological research on Christian conversion, Patricia Davis and Lewis Rambo highlight the importance of the metaphor of journey.[5] To undergo a conversion is, metaphorically, to move. But they note two distinct sub-types of the journey metaphor. The first, "a Christian life is walking a straight and narrow path" implies that conversion is a temporary transition from one stable meaning system to another stable meaning system. Once that transition is complete, the metaphor implies that the Christian life should be characterized by confidence, certainty about progress, and a refusal to deviate. The second metaphor, "a Christian life is walking a labyrinth" implies that the path is narrow and winding and constantly twisting and turning in unexpected and unpredictable directions. This metaphor suggests that the spiritual life is characterized by a state of continual openness to change, of "converting" as an ongoing process rather than "conversion" as a singular event.

In converting to a life that is more respectfully integrated into the ecosystems of which we are a part, the journey we need to make will be less like walking a straight path and more like walking the narrow and twisting path of a labyrinth. For as we seek to leave behind economic, technological, and religious practices that are destructive of the ecosystems on which we depend, it is not at all clear what new practices will sustain us. We need to embark on a journey whose destination is not clear. We will need to change and change again, trusting that even dead ends will still help us in the process of our transformation. If the turning spoken of in the old Shaker hymn can stand for our transformation, then it may indeed be that "to turn, turn will be our delight, 'til by turning, turning, we come round right."

Endnotes

Introduction

1 See the study *Toxic Wastes and Race* published by The United Church of Christ Commission for Racial Justice (1987), which first documented what has come to be called "environmental racism"; summarized in Rasmussen, *Earth Community, Earth Ethics,* 75–6.

2 Josué de Castro, quoted in Tony Brun, "Social Ecology: A Timely Paradigm for Reflection and Praxis for Life in Latin America"; in Hallman, *EcoTheology: Voices from South and North,* 82.

3 "The Human Person, the Heart of Peace," Jan. 1, 2007, par. #8.

4 Berry, *The Great Work: Our Way into the Future* (New York: Bell Tower, 1999).

5 Korten, *The Great Turning: From Empire to Earth Community* (San Francisco: Berrett-Koehler Publishers, Inc. and Bloomfield, CT: Kumarian Press, Inc., 2006). Korten derived the phrase from Joanna Macy's Web page titled "The Great Turning," http://www.joannamacy.net/html/great.html.

6 The phrase and image is that of William James.

Chapter 1

1 Lester Brown, *Plan B 3.0,* 4.

2 The story was told by Alanna Mitchell on the CBC radio program "The Current," March 4, 2009. See also her book *Sea Sick: The Global Ocean in Crisis.*

3 Scientists have already measured a worldwide long-term decline in phytoplankton levels in the world's oceans of approximately 40% between 1960 and 2010. Declines were measured in eight of the world's ten ocean regions, and seem to be at least partially correlated with increased ocean surface temperatures related to climate change. Increased surface temperatures are believed to lead to a greater stratification of ocean layers, which reduces the amount of nutrients available to phytoplankton. See Boyce et al., "Global phytoplankton decline over the past century," 591.

4 I have been unable to trace the source of this story. Even if it is apocryphal, the phenomenon it describes is undoubtedly real: even a very limited ecosystem is indescribably complex.

5 The following summary of the development of ecosystem theory is based on Des Jardins, *Environmental Ethics,* 167–173.

6 This description of thresholds and non-linear behaviour is indebted to Thomas Homer-Dixon's fine book, *The Upside of Down,* 24ff.

7 See Figure 1 in Roughgarden and Smith, "Why fisheries collapse," 5078.

8 Millenium Ecosystem Assessment, "Living Beyond Our Means," 15.

9 Diamond, *Collapse,* 489.

10 Garrett Hardin, "The Tragedy of the Commons."

11 Haas et al., eds., *Institutions for the Earth: Sources of Effective International Environmental Protection,* evaluates the success of international agreements on ozone, acid rain, water pollution, fisheries management, and population control.

12 Eric T. Freyfogle, "Private Property Rights in Land: An Agrarian View," 252–253.

13 See, to give only two examples, Elinor Ostrom, *Governing the Commons: The Evolution of Institutions for Collective Action,* and Daniel W. Bromley, ed. *Making the Commons Work: Theory, Practice, and Policy.*

14 These principles are summarized from the work of Elinor Ostrom, *Governing the Commons,* 88–102; and Ostrom, "The Rudiments of a Theory of the Origins, Survival and Performance of Common Property Institutions," 297–299, in Bromley, ed., *Making the Commons Work.*

15 Pope Benedict XVI, "The Human Person, the Heart of Peace," para. #8.

16 Lopez, "The Naturalist," n.p.

17 The full quote is "Economic theory for managing a renewable resource, such as a fishery, leads to an ecologically unstable equilibrium as difficult to maintain as balancing a marble on top of a dome. A fishery should be managed for ecological stability instead – in the analogy, as easy to maintain as keeping a marble near the base of a bowl." Roughgarden and Smith, "Why fisheries collapse," 5078.

18 Stevens, William K., "Biologists Fear Sustainable Yield Is Unsustainable Idea" citing an paper by Donald Ludwig, Carl Walters, Ray Hilborn in *Science,* April 2, 1993.

19 Thomas Homer-Dixon's book *The Upside of Down* is an extended argument that societies should focus more on resilience rather than economic efficiency.

20 More than one person has pointed out to me that this image is based on an unfair stereotype of cowboys, who are often sensitively attuned to the ecosystems on which they depend!

21 Rasmussen, *Earth Community, Earth Ethics.*

22 It seems odd to me that political organizations and parties labelled "conservative" are the least committed to conservation, the most suspicious of effective government or international regulation, and the most willing to entrust the health of natural systems to the working of a free market. Modern conservative parties and policies are more accurately described as neo-liberal. This is ironic given the way in which many conservatives deride liberalism.

Chapter 2

1 From The *Westminster Collection of Christian Prayers,* ed. Dorothy M. Stewart (Louisville: Westminster John Knox, 2002), 6; line breaks added by Davis, *Scripture, Culture, and Agriculture,* 47.

2 Summarized from http://marinebio.org/species.asp?id=302. Downloaded September 26, 2008.

3 Pierre-Yves Daoust et al., "Animal welfare and the harp seal hunt in Atlantic Canada," *The Canadian Veterinary Journal* 43 (9), 687–694; cited in http://en.wikipedia.org/wiki/Hakapik, downloaded September 19, 2008. The Canadian government's most recent regulations require that the hunter ensure the skull has been crushed and sever two arteries and allow it to bleed for a minimum of one minute to ensure it is dead.

4 These descriptions of ethical theory are based in large part on the helpful discussion in Des Jardins, *Environmental Ethics,* 15–36 and 137–139. Additional sources are noted in the text.

5 The illustration is drawn from Alisdair MacIntyre, *After Virtue.*

6 Aristotle, *Nichomachean Ethics,* 4.1, 71ff.

7 I am indebted for this point to Hauerwas and Berkman, "The Chief End of All Flesh," 202–3.

8   This illustration is drawn from Des Jardins, *Environmental Ethics*, 25.
9   Mill, *Utilitarianism*, 10.
10 Tom Regan, *The Case for Animal Rights*.
11 World Health Organization statistics find that the health outcomes of people in the bottom quintile of wealthy countries are approximately equal to those of the top quintile of developing countries. In other words, the best outcomes in developing countries only are as good as the worst outcomes in developed countries.
12 Putnam, *Bowling Alone*, 15–16.
13 *Democracy in America*, trans. George Lawrence, ed. J. P. Mayer (originally published 1835, 1840, New York: Doubleday, Anchor Books, 1969), 506, 508; quoted and summarized in Bellah et al., *Habits of the Heart*, 37.
14 Bellah et al., *Habits of the Heart*, 82.

Chapter 3

1   Leopold, *A Sand County Almanac*, 225.
2   Adapted from Aristotle, *Nicomachean Ethics*, Terence Irwin, trans. (Indianapolis/Cambridge: Hackett Publishing Company, 1985); see for example 1105b 6–9: "actions are called just or temperate when they are the sort that a just or temperate person would do. But the just and temperate person is not the one who [merely] does these actions, but the one who also does them in the way in which just and temperate people do them."
3   Steven Bouma-Prediger, *For the Beauty of the Earth*, 141–159.
4   "Tall Tales and Tiny Revolutions," *Sojourners*, November 2008, 9.
5   "On Not Winning the Nobel Prize," December 7, 2007; downloaded December 2, 2008 from http://nobelprize.org/nobel_prizes/literature/laureates/2007/lessing-lecture_en.html.
6   Alisdair MacIntyre, *After Virtue*, 222.
7   Driver, *Liberating Rites*, 213.
8   Barbara Brown Taylor, *The Luminous Web: Essays on Science and Religion* (Cambridge, Massachusetts: Cowley Publications, 2000), 74.
9   Albert Schweitzer, *Out of My Life and Thought*, trans. C. T. Campion (New York: Henry Holt and Company, 1949), 124.
10 Ibid. 126.
11 Ibid. 126.
12 Aldo Leopold, *A Sand County Almanac* , 130.
13 Ibid. 132.
14 Ibid. 215.
15 Ibid. viii.
16 Ibid. 207–8.
17 Ibid. Leopold, 225.
18 Ibid. 224–5.
19 J. Baird Callicott has proposed that Leopold's Land Ethic should be reinterpreted within the tradition of moral sentiments identified with David Hume. See the description of Callicott's thesis in Des Jardins, *Environmental Ethics*, 201–206.
20 Leopold, *A Sand County Almanac*, 6.
21 Ibid. 178.
22 Ibid. 225.
23 Stanley Hauerwas and John Berkman, "The Chief End of All Flesh," 197.

Chapter 4

1   "For God So Loved the Dirt," in *Sojourners*, Vol. 40, No. 4 (April 2011), 16.

2   I am grateful to my friend Russel Burns, a tribal member of the James Smith Cree Nation in Treaty Six Territory, for drawing this prophecy to my attention.

3   Quoted in Shinn, *Forced Options*, 112.

4   The phrase is that of Thomas Homer-Dixon, *The Ingenuity Gap*, 29ff and 234ff.

5   Julian Simon, *The Ultimate Resource* (Princeton, N.J.: Princeton University Press, 1981), 345; quoted in Homer-Dixon, *The Ingenuity Gap*, 234.

6   For a look at how China's growth will affect resource consumption, see Brown, *Plan B 3.0*, 13–14.

7   Ransom A. Myers and Boris Worm, "Rapid Worldwide Depletion of Predatory Fish Communities," *Nature*, vol. 432 (15 May 2003), 280–83; cited in Brown, *Plan B 3.0*.

8   The metaphor is that of Charles Birch, "Creation, Technology and Human Survival," 75.

9   I am indebted for the following insights to Thomas Homer-Dixon, *The Ingenuity Gap*, 33.

10 See Thomas Homer-Dixon, *The Ingenuity Gap*, 247–277 for a careful examination of this issue.

11 The World Bank reports that financial crises have become worse over the past thirty years. Between the late 1970s and the year 2000, 93 countries had 112 systemic banking crises. "These crises both were more numerous and expensive, compared with those earlier in history, and their costs often devastating in developing countries." World Bank, *Finance for Growth: Policy Choices in a Volatile World* (Washington, DC: World Bank, 2001), 75; cited in Homer-Dixon, *The Upside of Down*, 181.

12 "The Rotarian Conversation: Bill Gates" in *The Rotarian*, May 2009, 54. Interview by David Rensin.

13 According to "The Cocoyoc Declaration" of UNEP/UNCTAD in 1974, "Its methods are well known: the purposive maintenance of built-in bias of the existing market mechanisms, other forms of economic manipulation, withdrawing or withholding credits, embargoes, economic sanctions, subversive use of intelligence agencies, repression including torture, counter-insurgence operations, even full-scale intervention."

14 Sunita Narain, "Foreword," in *State of the World 2006* (New York: W. W. Norton & Company, 2006), xix.

15 World Bank, *Global Economic Prospects 2005: Trade Regionalism, and Development* (Washington, DC: World Bank, 2005), 21–22; quoted in Homer-Dixon, *The Upside of Down*, 186. The World Bank uses a method of calculating incomes which corrects for differences in purchasing power among various countries.

16 UNICEF, *The State of the World's Children 2005: Childhood under Threat* (New York: UNICEF, 2004), 19–22; quoted in Homer-Dixon, *The Upside of Down*, 186–7.

17 Luisa Kroll and Alison Fass, "The World's Billionaires," *Forbes*, March 9, 2006; quoted in Homer-Dixon, *The Upside of Down*, 187, 365 n. 34.

18 Quoted in Joseph R. Des Jardins, *Environmental Ethics*, 232–3.

19 On this point see Des Jardins, *Environmental Ethics*, 52–3.

20 Adapted from Clifford Cobb, Ted Halstead, and Jonathan Rowe, "If the GDP is Up, Why is America Down?" *The Atlantic Monthly*, October 1995, 59–78. See page 65.

21 Starting in the year 2000, a movement of students called for a "post-autistic economics." The movement began at the Sorbonne in France and spread rapidly to universities in England, the United States and other countries. Online at http://www.paecon.net/. The term "autism" to describe a blindness to ecological concerns was used earlier by Thomas Berry, *The Dream of Earth* (San Francisco: Sierra Club Books,1988), 16. I am indebted to my student Sally Floden for drawing my attention to this quotation.

22 Lester R. Brown, *Eco-Economy: Building an Economy for the Earth* (New York: W. W. Norton & Company, Inc., 2001), 3–4.

23 Costanza, Bob, et al., "The value of the world's ecosystem services and natural capital," *Nature* 387, 253–260 (15 May 1997); online at http://www.nature.com/nature/journal/v387/n6630/abs/387253a0.html.

24 For a careful analysis of this point by an interdisciplinary group of environmentalists and ecologists, see Kenneth Arrow et al., "Are We Consuming Too Much?" *Journal of Economic Perspectives*, vol. 18, no. 3 (September 2003), 147–72. "High levels of consumption in rich countries may promote excessive resource degradation in poor countries, which imperils well-being in the poorer countries" (p. 166). Online at http://pubs.aeaweb.org/doi/pdfplus/10.1257/0895330042162377.

25 Herman Daly, "Sustainable Growth: An Impossibility Theorem," reprinted in *Valuing the Earth,* eds. Herman Daly and Kenneth Townsend (Boston: Massachusetts Institute of Technology Press, 1993), 267–8; quoted in Des Jardins, *Environmental Ethics*, 61.

26 "The Real Cost of Gasoline: Report No. 3: An Analysis of the Hidden External Costs Consumers Pay to Fuel Their Automobiles," downloaded February 19, 2011 from http://www.icta.org/doc/Real%20Price%20of%20Gasoline.pdf. See also Lester Brown, *Plan B 3.0*, 267ff.

27 Factual information on the Marlin mine is available on the Goldcorp website: http://www.goldcorp.com/operations/marlin/. In 2008, under pressure from shareholders from socially responsible investment groups, Goldcorp agreed to an independent Human Rights Impact Assessment, documents from which can be found at http://www.hria-guatemala.com/en/default.htm. The activities of Goldcorp and other Canadian mining companies are monitored by the non-governmental organization Mining Watch Canada and its partners. See www.miningwatch.ca.

28 I have withheld Christina's full name because of human rights violations against opponents of the mine, a tragically common occurrence in Guatemala. On July 7, 2010 another active critic of the mine was shot in the head.

29 Cathy Hoshour points out that even the 15 million figure may be too low because it only counts the direct displacement and does not factor in the indirect effect of environmental damage. See "Multiplying Displacement Impacts: Development as Usual in a Changing Global Climate," paper presented at the 15th Annual International Metropolis Conference in The Hague, Netherlands, October 4–8, 2010. Online at http://www.metropolis2010.org//docs/Metropolis/katehoshourpaper.pdf.

30 The speech is available on the website of the Harry S. Truman Library & Museum. See http://www.trumanlibrary.org/whistlestop/50yr_archive/inagural20jan1949.htm.

31 Bruce Rich, *Mortgaging the Earth: The World Bank, Environmental Impoverishment, and the Crisis of Development* (Boston: Beacon Press, 1995), n.p.; quoted in Rasmussen, *Earth Community, Earth Ethics*, 43.

32 Quoted in Cobb, et al., "If the GDP is Up, Why is America Down?" 68.

33 Cited in McKibben, *Deep Economy*.

34 Quoted in Cobb, et al., "If the GDP is Up, Why is America Down?" 68. Since that assessment, Indonesia has continued to grow rapidly, but was hard hit by the Asian financial crisis in 1997–8 and has grown more slowly since.

35 McKibben, *Deep Economy*, 28.

36 David A. Holmes, "Sabbath Practice as a Resistance to Consumerism: A Lenten Experiment in Congregational Sabbath Practice," unpublished D.Min. Project Report (Decatur, Georgia: Columbia Theological Seminary, 2008), 1.

37 McKibben, *Deep Economy*, 36.

38 Mark Anielski, "The Genuine Progress Indicator – A Principled Approach to Economics," *Encompass*, October/November 1999. Online at http://pubs. pembina.org/reports/gpi_economics.pdf. August 25, 2009.

Chapter 5

1 Wendell Berry, *Life Is a Miracle*, 7.

2 Barry Lopez, *Of Wolves and Men*, 284.

3 For thoughtful critiques of this view, see Wendell Berry, *Life Is a Miracle*, 46ff, and Maria Mies, "Feminist Research."

4 Descartes, *Discourse on Method*, 1637.

5 "Splicing Life: A Report on the Social and Ethical Issues of Genetic Engineering with Human Beings," by the President's Commission for the Study of Ethical Problems in Medicine and Biomedical Research, 1982, 56, quoted by Granberg-Michaelson, *A Worldly Spirituality*, 196.

6 Martin Heidegger, "The Question Concerning Technology."

7 Charles Birch, "Creation, Technology and Human Survival," 78.

8 Barry Lopez, *Of Wolves and Men*, 284.

9 Preface to *Psychopannychia*, trans. Henry Beveridge, *Tracts and Treatises in Defense of the Reformed Faith*, vol. 3 (Grand Rapids: Eerdmans, 1958), 418; quoted in Davis, *Scripture, Culture and Agriculture*, 34.

10 I am indebted for this way of seeing the matter to Jacques Derrida, "The Principle of Reason."

11 "Technological Detoxification," pp. 302–307 in *Faith and Science in an Unjust World*, Vol. 1: Plenary Presentations, ed. Roger L. Shinn (Geneva: World Council of Churches, 1980), 304.

12 This point is made by Dr. Dianna Manning, a scientist at Middlesex Polytechnic in England, quoted in Kerstin Anér, "Community Involvement in Scandinavian Decisions," 337–341 in *Faith and Science in an Unjust World*, 339. I think this way of putting the matter is problematic, as it seems to me that the fallacy is the assumption that men *are* able to cut themselves off from other aspects of life.

13 Jacques Ellul, *Perspectives on Our Age*, ed. William H. Vanderburg, trans. Joachim Neugroshel (New York: The Seabury Press, 1981), 49.

14 Huston Smith, "Technology and Human Values: This American Moment," in *Human Values and Advancing Technology* 23–24.

15 See Ellul, *The Technological Society* (New York: Vintage Books, 1967).

16 See Postman, *Technopoly: The Surrender of Culture to Technology* (New York: Vintage Books, 1993).

17 Galbraith, *The New Industrial State* (Houghton-Mifflin, 1971), n.p.; quoted in Charles Susskind, *Understanding Technology*, 88.

18 I am thinking here of skepticism about human-caused climate change. Scientific research is by its nature critical in thought, and that is an important contribution to the method, but careful critical thought is a very different matter from dismissing a conclusion supported by significant evidence simply because we find it inconvenient or uncomfortable.

19 This approach is found throughout Lopez's book *Of Wolves and Men*. I am grateful to my teacher Romand Coles for drawing my attention to the work of Lopez. See Coles, "Ecotones and Environmental Ethics: Adorno and Lopez," in *In the Nature of Things*, 231.

20 Wes Jackson, "Introduction," in *The Virtues of Ignorance: Complexity, Sustainability and the Limits of Knowledge*, by Bill Vitek and Wes Jackson (Lexington: The University Press of Kentucky, 2008), 1; quoted in Davis, *Scripture, Culture and Agriculture*, 33.

21 Wes Jackson, *Becoming Native to this Place* (Lexington: University Press of Kentucky, 1994), 23; quoted in Davis, *Scripture, Culture and Agriculture*, 33–4.

22 *Scripture, Culture and Agriculture*, 34

23 Benyus, *Biomimicry*, 287–295.

Chapter 6

1 "How to Be a Poet," *Poetry* (January 2001); online at http://poetry foundation.org/archive/poem.html?id=30299.

2 The Letter is available from several online sources, including The National Religious Partnership for the Environment: http://www.nrpe.org/statements/ interfaith_statmts_a01.htm.

3 Holmes, "Sabbath Practice as a Resistance to Consumerism, 9–10.

4 Charles Birch and Paul Abrecht, eds., *Genetics and the Quality of Life* (Oxford: Pergamon, 1975), 203; quoted in Birch, "Creation, Technology and Human Survival," 76–77.

5 *The One-Straw Revolution: An Introduction to Natural Farming*, ed. Larry Korn (Emmaus, Pa.: Rodale, 1978), 25–26; quoted in Davis, *Scripture, Culture and Agriculture*, 179.

6 Theodor Adorno, *Negative Dialectics*, 162.

7 *Negative Dialectics*, 162.

8 The phrase is adapted from Catherine Keller's comment that what we need is "ecumenism of the mind and hence a pluralistic epistemology...," in "Chosen Persons and the Green Ecumenacy: A Possible Christian Response to the Population Apocalypse," pp. 300–311, in David Hallman, *Ecotheology*, 310.

9 Steven Bouma-Prediger, for example, although he considers respect for the well-being and integrity of other creatures a virtue, considers reverence as an excess of "inflated regard" for other creatures and therefore a vice: "Reverence in this sense is misplaced regard in which someone worships a creature or creation as a whole rather than the Creator." *For the Beauty of the Earth*, 143.

10 Gore, *Earth in the Balance*, 12.

11 Ibid. 258.

12 Lynn White, Jr., "The Historical Roots of our Ecological Crisis," *Science*, 123–127.

13 Wendell Berry, "Foreward," in Davis, *Scripture, Culture and Agriculture*," xiii.

14 Ibid.

15 Howard Becker, "Processes of Secularization: An Ideal-Typical Analysis with Special Reference to Personality Change as Affected by Population Movement," *The Sociological Review*, Vol. XXIV (1932), 138–154, 266–286; this summary of Becker's findings is drawn from Birch and Rasmussen, *Predicament of the Prosperous*, 110–1.

16 The use of miles, rather than kilometres, is intentional. Although Canada converted to the metric system decades ago, the land is still divided in "sections" one mile square, and road allowances are miles, not kilometres apart.

17 Davis, *Scripture, Culture and Agriculture*, 22.

18 *The Unsettling of America: Culture and Agriculture* (San Fransisco: Sierra Club, 1977), 31; quoted in Davis, *Scripture, Culture and Agriculture*, 108.

19 There has been a vigorous discussion in ecumenical circles over the merits and dangers of using stewardship as a dominant model of the human vocation. See the exploration of the issue in Larry Rasmussen, *Earth Community, Earth Ethics*, 230–236.

Chapter 7

1   Tom F. Driver, *Liberating Rites*, 183–4

2   Ibid. For this summary of Driver's work, I have drawn extensively on David A. Holmes, "Sabbath Practice as a Resistance to Consumerism," 10–14.

3   The phrase is one commonly used by John Calvin. See the study by Susan Schreiner, *The Theater of His Glory: Nature and the Natural Order in the Thought of John Calvin*, Studies in Historical Theology 3.

4   1 Corinthians 14:8

5   Driver, *Liberating Rites*, 200.

6   Quoted in Wink, *Engaging the Powers*, 196–7.

7   Tom F. Driver, *Liberating Rites*, 172.

8   Wink, *Unmasking the Powers*, 64.

9   The story is recounted in Douglas John Hall, *Imaging God: Dominion as Stewardship*, 204.

10 Jürgen Moltmann, *God in Creation*, 71.

11 Ibid. 71.

12 St. Francis of Assisi (circa 1225 CE), English translation William Henry Draper (circa 1919 CE), "All Creatures of Our God and King" (New York: Boosey and Hawkes); *Voices United*, #217, verses. 1, 3.

13 Ruth Duck, "It's a Song of Praise to the Maker," verses 1 & 4 (Chicago: GIA Publications, 1992); in *More Voices* (Toronto: United Church Publishing House; Kelowna: Wood Lake Books; Louisville: Westminster John Knox Press, 2007), #30.

14 Wendell Berry, Postscript to "The Landscaping of Hell: Strip-Mine Morality in East Kentucky" from *The Long-Legged House;* online at http://being.publicradio.org/programs/2010/land-life-poetry/essay_postscript.shtml.

15 Bruce Cockburn, "If a Tree Falls in a Forest," in *Big Circumstance* (True North Records, 1988).

16 Confession from the liturgy "River Sunday 2 (USA)," from *Season of Creation* website, downloaded February 19, 2011 from http://seasonofcreation.com/wp-content/uploads/2010/04/liturgy-usa-river-sunday-2.pdf.

17 Psalm 44, for example, contains a protest that what is happening is not fair and is undeserved: "All this has happened despite our loyalty to you. We have not violated your covenant. Our hearts have not deserted you. We have not strayed from your path. Yet you have crushed us in the desert. You have covered us with darkness and death." (Psalm 44:17–19, NLT) The psalm then goes on to complain that God has not been paying adequate attention: "Wake up, O Lord! Why do you sleep? Get up! Do not reject us forever. Why do you look the other way? Why do you ignore our suffering and oppression?" (Psalm 44:23–24, NLT)

18 Shirley Erena Murray, "God Weeps" (Hope Publishing Company, 1996); in *More Voices*, #78, vs. 1, 3.

Chapter 8

1 Quoted in Rasmussen, *Earth Community, Earth Ethics*, 179; original reference not cited.
2 *Terminator 2: Judgement Day* (Lionsgate, 1991).
3 Paraphrased from Moltmann's lecture "Living a Theology of Hope Today."
4 The phrase "participatory hope" is adapted from "participatory eschatology," a phrase used by John Dominic Crossan in a lecture at the Epiphany Explorations Conference, Victoria, B.C., January 2008.
5 "Letter from a Birmingham Jail," 280.
6 In an interview on Mansbridge One on One, CBC Newsworld, March 5, 2011.
7 Yordy, *Green Witness*, 13.
8 Ibid., 131, note 1; see also the Facebook page of Koinonia Farm, http://www.facebook.com/koinoniafarm#!/koinoniafarm; downloaded February 5, 2011.
9 "Koinonia Farms: An Introductory History;" online at http://www.koinonia partners.org/History/brief.html; downloaded February 5, 2011.
10 For a history of this development, see Doris L. Bergen, *The Twisted Cross*.
11 The phrase comes from the title of Elizabeth O'Connor's book telling the story of the Church of the Saviour in Washington, D.C., which is a good example of an anticipatory community, although it is not focused on issues of sustainability.
12 Birch & Rasmussen, *Predicament of the Prosperous*, 187.
13 Yordy, *Green Witness*, 152.
14 Ibid. 152.
15 Wirzba, "For God So Loved the Dirt," 18.
16 Brueggemann, *The Land*, 63.
17 Abraham Joshua Heschel, *The Sabbath* (New York: Farrar, Straus and Giroux, 1951), 23; quoted in Holmes, "Sabbath Practice as a Resistance to Consumerism," 14.
18 Holmes, "Sabbath Practice as a Resistance to Consumerism," 14.
19 I use this expression to emphasize that the church is not primarily an institution but a social movement, defined less by its structure than by its objective of witness to God's kingdom.
20 Wendell Berry, untitled poem, *A Timbered Choir*, 18.
21 Quoted without original reference in Brun, "Social Ecology" p. 84; in Hallman, *Ecotheology*.
22 W. O. Mitchell, *Jake and the Kid*, 100–1.

Conclusion

1 Romans 7:15, 18–19, NRSV.
2 The phrase is from singer/songwriter Bruce Cockburn's lament for the rain forest, "If a Tree Falls in a Forest."
3 Wangari Maathai "Our Environment, Our Future."
4 Berry, *The Great Work*, 3.
5 Patricia Davis and Lewis Rambo, "Converting: Toward a Cognitive Theory of Religious Change," 159–173.

Bibliography

Adorno, Theodor. *Negative Dialectics*. Trans. E. B. Ashton. New York: Continuum, 1973.

Alter, Jonathan. "He Only Saved a Billion People." *Newsweek*. July 30, 2007.

Anahareo. *Grey Owl and I*. London: Peter Davies, 1972.

Anielski, Mark. "The Genuine Progress Indicator – A Principled Approach to Economics." *Encompass* (October/November 1999). Downloaded August 25, 2009 from http://pubs. pembina.org/reports/gpi economics.pdf.

Aristotle. *Nichomachean Ethics*. Trans. Terence Irwin. Indianapolis, Indiana: Hackett Publishing Company, 1985.

Arrow, Kenneth, et al. "Are We Consuming Too Much?" *Journal of Economic Perspectives*, vol. 18, no. 3 (September 2003), 147–72. Online at http://pubs.aeaweb.org/doi/pdfplus/ 10.1257/0895330042162377.

Bass, Diana Butler. *Christianity for the Rest of Us: How the Neighborhood Church Is Transforming the Faith*. New York: HarperCollins Publishers, 2006.

Bellah, Robert N., Richard Madsen, William M. Sullivan, Ann Swidler, and Steven M. Tipton. *Habits of the Heart: Individualism and Commitment in American Life*. Berkeley: University of California Press, 1985.

Bergen, Doris L. *The Twisted Cross: The German Christian Movement in the Third Reich*. Chapel Hill: University of North Carolina Press, 1996.

Berry, Thomas. *The Dream of the Earth*. San Francisco: Sierra Club Books,1988.

———. *The Great Work: Our Way into the Future*. New York: Bell Tower, 1999.

Berry, Wendell. *Life Is a Miracle: An Essay Against Modern Superstition*. Washington, D.C.: Counterpoint, 2001.

———. *A Timbered Choir: The Sabbath Poems 1979–1997*. New York: Counterpoint, 1998.

Billinghurst, Jane. *Grey Owl: The Many Faces of Archie Belaney*. Vancouver/Toronto: Greystone Books, 1999.

Birch, Bruce and Larry Rasmussen. *The Predicament of the Prosperous*. Biblical Perspectives on Current Issues. Philadelphia: The Westminster Press, 1978.

Birch, Charles. "Creation, Technology and Human Survival." *Ecumenical Review* 28 (January 1976), 66–79.

Bouma-Prediger, Steven. *For the Beauty of the Earth: A Christian Vision for Creation Care*. Grand Rapids: Baker Academic, 2001.

Boyce, Daniel G., Marlon R. Lewis & Boris Worm. "Global phytoplankton decline over the past century." *Nature* 466, (29 July 2010), 591–596.

Bromley, Daniel W. Ed. *Making the Commons Work: Theory, Practice, and Policy*. San Francisco: Institute for Contemporary Studies Press, 1992.

Brown, Lester R. *Eco-Economy: Building an Economy for the Earth*. New York: W. W. Norton & Company, Inc., 2001.

———. "Nature's Limits," in Brown et al. *State of the World 1995: A Worldwatch Institute Report on Progress Toward a Sustainable Society*. New York: W. W. Norton & Company, 1995.

———. *Plan B 3.0: Mobilizing to Save Civilization*. Earth Policy Institute. W. W. Norton & Company, 2008.

————. *World on the Edge: How to Prevent Environmental and Economic Collapse*. Earth Policy Institute. W. W. Norton & Company, 2011.

Brueggemann, Walter. *The Land: Place as Gift, Promise, and Challenge in Biblical Faith*. Minneapolis: Fortress Press, 1977.

Brun, Tony. "Social Ecology: A Timely Paradigm for Reflection and Praxis for Life in Latin America," in Hallman, *Ecotheology*. 79–91.

Cayley, David. *The Age of Ecology: The Environment on CBC Radio's Ideas*. Toronto: James Lorimer & Company, 1991.

Cobb, Clifford, Ted Halstead, and Jonathan Rowe. "If the GDP is Up, Why is America Down?" *The Atlantic Monthly* (October 1995), 59–78.

Coles, Ronald. "Economics and Environmental Ethics: Adorno and Lopez," in *The Nature of Things*, ed. Jane Bennett and William Chaloupka. Minneapolis: University of Minnesota Press.

Costanza, Bob, et al., "The value of the world's ecosystem services and natural capital." *Nature* 387 (15 May 1997), 253–260; abstract online at http://www.nature.com/nature/journal/v387/n6630/abs/387253a0.html.

Daly, Herman. "Sustainable Growth: An Impossibility Theorem." In *Valuing the Earth*. Eds. Herman Daly and Kenneth Townsend. Boston: Massachusetts Institute of Technology Press, 1993; 267–8.

Davis, Ellen F. *Scripture, Culture and Agriculture: An Agrarian Reading of the Bible*. Cambridge University Press, 2009.

Davis, Patricia and Lewis Rambo. "Converting: Toward a Cognitive Theory of Religious Change." In Kelly Bulkeley, editor. *Soul, Psyche, Brain: New Directions in the Study of Religion and Brain-Mind Science*. New York: Palgrave Macmillan, 2005.

Derrida, Jacques. "The Principle of Reason: The University in the Eyes of its Pupils." trans. Catherine Porter and Edward P. Morris, *Diacritics*, Fall 1983, 3-20.

Des Jardins, Joseph R. *Environmental Ethics: An Introduction to Environmental Philosophy*, Third Edition. Stamford, CT: Wadsworth, 2001.

Diamond, Jared. *Collapse: How Societies Choose to Fail or Succeed*. New York: Viking, 2005.

————. *Guns, Germs and Steel*. New York: W. W. Norton & Company, 1999.

————. *The Third Chimpanzee*. New York: Harper Perennial, 2005.

Dickson, Lovat. *Wilderness Man: The Strange Story of Grey Owl*. Toronto: Macmillan of Canada, 1973.

Diehl, William. *The Monday Connection: A Spirituality of Competence, Affirmation and Support in the Workplace*. New York: HarperCollins, 1991.

Diener, Ed, and Martin Seligman. "Beyond Money: Toward an Economy of Well-Being." *Psychological Science in the Public Interest*. Vol. 5. No. 1 (July 2004). Online at http://www.psychologicalscience.org/pdf/pspi/pspi5_1.pdf.

Driver, Tom F. *Liberating Rites: Understanding the Transformative Power of Ritual*. Boulder, Colorado: Westview Press, 1998.

Flavin, Christopher. "Preface," in Worldwatch Institute, *State of the World 2005: Redefining Global Security*. New York: W. W. Norton & Company, 2005.

Freyfogle, Eric T. "Private Property Rights in Land: An Agrarian View," in Norman Wirzba, ed. *The Essential Agrarian Reader: The Future of Culture, Community, and the Land*. Lexington: University Press of Kentucky, 2003, 237–258.

Gibson, Stacey. "The Lives of Animals." *University of Toronto Magazine*. Autumn, 2010. 40–43.

Gore, Al Jr. *Earth in the Balance: Ecology and the Human Spirit*. New York: Penguin Group, 1993.

Granberg-Michaelson, Wesley. *A Worldly Spirituality: The Call to Redeem Life on Earth*. New York: Harper & Row, 1984.

———. "Creation in Ecumenical Theology." Pages 96–106 in David Hallman, editor. *Ecotheology: Voices from South and North*. Maryknoll, N.Y.: Orbis Books; and Geneva: WCC Publications, 1994.

Grey Owl. *Pilgrims of the Wild*. London: Peter Davies, 1935; Toronto: Macmillan Paperbacks, 1990.

———. *The Men of the Last Frontier*. Toronto: Macmillan of Canada, 1931.

———. *Tales of an Empty Cabin*. Toronto: Macmillan of Canada, 1936.

Haas, Peter M., Robert O. Keohane, and Marc A. Levy. *Institutions for the Earth: Sources of Effective International Environmental Protection*. Cambridge, Massachusetts and London, England: The MIT Press, 1993.

Hall, Douglas John. *Imaging God: Dominion as Stewardship*. Grand Rapids: Wm. B. Eerdmans Publishing Co, New York: Friendship Press, 1986.

Hallman, David G. *EcoTheology: Voices from South and North*. Geneva: WCC Press, and Maryknoll, N.Y.: Orbis Press, 1994.

Hardin, Garrett. "The Tragedy of the Commons." *Science*. Vol. 162 (1968), 1243–48.

Hauerwas, Stanley & John Berkman. "The Chief End of All Flesh," *Theology Today*, Vol. 49, No. 2 (July 1992).

Heidegger, Martin. "The Question Concerning Technology" (1953), in *Basic Writings*. Revised and Expanded Edition. Ed. David Farrell Krell. HarperSanFrancisco, 1993.

Heinlein, Robert A. *The Moon Is a Harsh Mistress*. New York. G.P. Putnam's Sons. New York. 1966.

Holmes, David A. "Sabbath Practice as a Resistance to Consumerism: A Lenten Experiment in Congregational Sabbath Practice." Unpublished D.Min. Project Report, Columbia Theological Seminary (Decatur, Georgia). 2008.

Homer-Dixon, Thomas. *The Ingenuity Gap: Can We Solve the Problems of the Future?* Toronto: Vintage Canada, 2001.

———. *The Upside of Down: Catastrophe, Creativity, and the Renewal of Civilization*. Toronto: Vintage Canada, 2007.

Hoshour, Cathy. "Multiplying Displacement Impacts: Development as Usual in a Changing Global Climate." Paper presented at the 15th Annual International Metropolis Conference in The Hague, Netherlands, October 4–8, 2010. Online at http://www.metropolis2010.org//docs/Metropolis/katehoshourpaper.pdf.

International Centre for Technology Assessment. "The Real Cost of Gasoline: Report No. 3: An Analysis of the Hidden External Costs Consumers Pay to Fuel Their Automobiles." Downloaded February 19, 2011 from http://www.icta.org/doc/Real%20Price%20of%20Gasoline.pdf.

IPCC, *Contribution of Working Group II to the Fourth Assessment Report of the Intergovernmental Panel on Climate Change*, 2007. Cambridge, United Kingdom and New York, NY, USA: Cambridge University Press, 2007. Downloaded March 30, 2011 from http://www.ipcc.ch/publications_and_data/ar4/wg2/en/ch5s5-4-2-2.html.

Kahn, Joseph and Jim Yardley. "Choking on Growth: As China rises, pollution soars," *New York Times*, August 25, 2007, downloaded December 18, 2008 from http://www.nytimes.com/2007/08/25/world/asia/25iht-26china.7254418.html?_r=1.

King, Martin Luther, Jr. "Letter from a Birmingham Jail." April 16, 1963. Reprinted in Flip Schulke and Penelope McPhee. *King Remembered*. New York: Pocket Books, 1986. 276–284.

Korten, David C. *The Great Turning: From Empire to Earth Community*. San Francisco: Berrett-Koehler Publishers, Inc. and Bloomfield, CT: Kumarian Press, Inc., 2006.

Leopold, Aldo. *A Sand County Almanac.* New York: Oxford University Press, 1949.

Lopez, Barry Holstun. *Of Wolves and Men.* New York: Charles Scribner's Sons, 1978.

———. "The Naturalist," in *Orion* (Autumn 2001). Downloaded January 28, 2011 from http://orionmagazine.org/index.php/articles/article/91/.

Maathai, Wangari. "Our Environment, Our Future: A Statement on the Occasion of District Conference & Assembly of Rotary District 9200." May 17, 2007. Downloaded September 11, 2008 from http://greenbeltmovement.org/a.php?id=238.

MacIntyre, Alisdair, *After Virtue: A Study in Moral Theory,* Second Edition. Notre Dame, Indiana: University of Notre Dame Press, 1984.

McClinton, Lorne. "The Energy Spend," in *The Furrow* (January 2011), Vol. 116, Issue 1, 10–13.

McKibben, Bill. *Deep Economy: The Wealth of Communities and the Durable Future.* New York: Holt Paperbacks, 2007.

Mies, Maria. "Feminist Research: Science, Violence and Responsibility." Pages 36–54 in Maria Mies & Vandana Shiva. *Ecofeminism.* Halifax: Fernwood Publications; London and New Jersey: Zed Books, 1993.

Mill, John Stuart. *Utilitarianism.* 1863. Indianapolis/Cambridge: Hackett Publishing Company, 1979.

Millenium Ecosystem Assessment. *Living Beyond Our Means: Natural Assets and Human Well-being: Statement from the Board.* Downloaded on December 4, 2010 from http://www.maweb.org/documents/document.429.aspx.pdf.

Mitchell, Alanna. *Sea Sick: The Global Ocean in Crisis.* Toronto: McClelland & Stewart, 2009.

Mitchell, W. O. *Jake and the Kid.* 1961. Toronto: Seal Books, 1982.

Moltmann, Jürgen. *God in Creation: A New Theology of Creation and the Spirit of God.* London: SCM, 1985, Minneapolis: Fortress Press, 1993.

———. "Living a Theology of Hope Today." Non-commercial sound recording in the library of St. Stephen's College, Edmonton. Circa 1989.

Narain, Sunita. "Foreword," in *State of the World* 2006. New York: W. W. Norton & Company, 2006.

Niebuhr, Reinhold. *Moral Man, Immoral Society.* New York: Charles Scribner's Sons, 1960.

O'Connor, Elizabeth. *Journey Inward, Journey Outward.* New York: Harper & Row, 1968.

Oreskes, Naomi. "Beyond the Ivory Tower: The Scientific Consensus on Climate Change." *Science,* Vol. 306, No. 5702 (2004), 1686.

Ostrom, Elinor. *Governing the Commons: The Evolution of Institutions for Collective Action.* Political Economy of Institutions and Decisions. Cambridge University Press, 1990.

Pollan, Michael. *The Omnivore's Dilemma: A Natural History of Four Meals.* New York: Penguin Books, 2006.

Pope Benedict XVI. "The Human Person, the Heart of Peace" Message for the Celebration of the World Day of Peace. Jan. 1, 2007. Downloaded April 4, 2011 from http://www.vatican.va/holy_father/benedict_xvi/messages/peace/documents/hf_ben-xvi_mes_20061208_xl-world-day-peace_en.html.

Putnam, Robert. *Bowling Alone: The Collapse and Revival of American Community.* New York: Touchstone Books, 2000.

Rasmussen, Larry. *Earth Community, Earth Ethics.* Maryknoll, N.Y.: Orbis Books, 1996.

Regan, Tom. *The Case for Animal Rights.* Berkeley: University of California Press, 1983.

Replogle, Jill. "Hunger on the Rise in Central America," *The Lancet,* Vol. 363 (June 19, 2004), 2057–8.

Roughgarden, Jonathan and Fraser Smith. "Why fisheries collapse and what to do about it," *Proceedings of the National Academy of Sciences* USA Vol. 93 (May 1996), 5078–5083. Available online at http://www.pnas.org/content/93/10/5078.full.pdf.

Scheffer, M. *The Ecology of Shallow Lakes.* London: Chapman and Hall, 1998.

Schreiner, Susan. *The Theater of His Glory: Nature and the Natural Order in the Thought of John Calvin.* Studies in Historical Theology 3. Durham, North Carolina: The Labyrinth Press, 1991.

Schweitzer, Albert. *Out of My Life and Thought.* Trans. C. T. Campion. New York: Henry Holt and Company, 1949.

Shinn, Roger Lincoln. *Forced Options: Social Decisions for the 21st Century.* San Francisco: Harper and Row, Publishers, 1982.

Smith, Donald B. *From the Land of Shadows: The Making of Grey Owl.* Saskatoon: Western Producer Prairie Books, 1990.

Smith, Huston. "Technology and Human Values: This American Moment." In *Human Values and Advancing Technology: A New Agenda for the Church in Mission.* Ed. Cameron P. Hall. New York: Friendship Press, 1967, 15–29.

Stevens, William K.. "Biologists Fear Sustainable Yield Is Unsustainable Idea." *New York Times.* April 2, 1993.

Susskind, Charles K. *Understanding Technology.* Baltimore/London: The John Hopkins University Press, 1973.

UNEP/UNCTAD Symposium on Patterns of Resource Use, Environment and Development Strategies. "The Cocoyoc Declaration." *Development Dialogue*, No. 2, 1974, 88–96.

White, Lynn Jr. "The Historical Roots of Our Ecological Crisis." *Science* Vol 155, No. 3767, (March 1967).

Wink, Walter. *Engaging the Powers: Discernment and Resistance in a World of Domination. The Powers*, Volume 3. Minneapolis: Fortress Press, 1992.

———. *Unmasking the Powers: The Invisible Forces that Determine Human Existence. The Powers*, Volume 2. Minneapolis: Fortress Press, 1986.

Wirzba, Norman, ed. *The Essential Agrarian Reader: The Future of Culture, Community, and the Land.* Lexington: University Press of Kentucky, 2003.

Wirzba, Norman. "For God So Loved the Dirt," in *Sojourners*, Vol. 40, No. 4 (April 2011).

Worster, David. *The Wealth of Nature.* New York: Oxford University Press, 1993.

Yardley, Jim. "After 30 years, economic perils on China's path," *International Herald Tribune*, Asia Pacific online edition, December 19, 2008. Downloaded December 18, 2008 from http://www.iht.com/articles/2008/12/19/asia/19china.php?page=2.

Index